MORE GREAT KIWI JOKES

MORE GREAT KIWI JOKES

Compiled by Sonya Plowman

Cartoons by Geoff Hocking

SUMMIT PRESS

SUMMIT
PRESS

22 Summit Road, Noble Park
Victoria 3174 Australia
Phone: +61 3 9790 5000
Fax: +61 3 9790 6888

First published 2002

© Summit Press

All rights reserved

Cartoons: Geoff Hocking

Edited by Samone Bos

Designed by SBR Productions Olinda Victoria

Printed in Australia by Griffin Press

National Library of Australia Cataloguing in Publication data

ISBN 1 86503 780 X

1. New Zealand wit and humour. 2. Wit and humour.
I. Hocking, Geoff, 1947-. II Plowman, Sonya, 1972-.

Contents

Blokes and Chicks	7
The Pope Walked Into a Bar One Day...	48
The Dumb, the Blonde, and the Irish	81
Naughty Stuff	128
Oddities	158
For Any Occasion	236

Blokes and Chicks

At Rangi's stag night his father raised a glass of beer and proposed a toast. 'To my son, on the happiest day of his life.'
'But, Dad,' said Rangi, 'I'm not getting married until tomorrow.'
The old man continued, 'I repeat, to my son...'

★ ★ ★

One day, a father and son were walking down the street when the boy saw a bee alight on the footpath in front of them. Immediately, the boy ran over and stomped on it. 'That was a precious honey bee,' said his father, shocked. 'For stomping on him and taking away his precious life you will do without honey for a week.'

They continued on down the road and the boy saw a butterfly, so he ran over and stomped on it.
'That was a butterfly,' his father said, 'one of nature's wonderful creatures, and for stomping him you will do without butter for a week.'
The next morning the family sat down for breakfast. The boy dejectedly ate his plain toast with no honey or butter. Suddenly, a cockroach ran out from under the fridge. His mother promptly stomped on the horrible creature.
The boy looked at his father and said, 'Are you going to tell her, Dad, or should I?'

★ ★ ★

A woman goes into a sex shop and asks if she can look at an assortment of vibrators. Despite the wide range of shapes and colours, none of them are the size that she wants.
'Listen here, pal,' she says to the man behind the counter, 'I've been around the traps and know exactly what I'm after. This selection is bloody pathet...' Suddenly she stops, and smiles, 'Well, hang on a minute! What about that big tartan one on the bottom shelf?'
'Sorry, ma'am,' replies the proprietor, 'that's my thermos flask.'

Blokes and Chicks

The king was rather annoyed that his daughter was going to marry his enemy's son. The wedding day went off without a hitch, but the king sent a spy to make sure his daughter was treated well on her wedding night. The next morning the spy met with the king to inform him of the previous night's goings-on.
'Well, my loyal servant, how did it go?' asked the king.
'Oh, wonderful, sir,' replied the spy. 'The first thing I heard was the princess saying, "My beloved husband, I offer you my honour" to which the prince responded, "My dear bride, I honour your offer."' The spy fell silent, and the king said, 'Yes? What else?'
'Nothing else,' replied the spy. 'That's how it was for the rest of the night – honour, offer, honour, offer.'

★ ★ ★

'So, do you want the bad news first or the terrible news?' the lawyer asked Mr Foley.
'Go on, shoot. Give me the bad news,' replied Mr Foley.
'The bad news is that your wife found a picture that's worth half a million dollars.'
'That's bad news?' asked Mr Foley. 'Well, what's the terrible news then?'
'The terrible news is that it's of you and your secretary.'

Mr Blitherington walked into a car dealership in Auckland, selected a hot pink BMW for his mistress, and lied to the salesman, 'Errm, it's for my wife.'
However, Mrs Blitherington happened to be passing by, so it was.

★ ★ ★

Jerry had a voracious sexual appetite and was never able to find satisfaction with his wife, so he had developed the nasty habit of having affairs. One day though, he confided to his best mate that he was going to confess to his wife and beg for her forgiveness. His best mate warned him not to reveal the names of the women, for, as he explained to Jerry, 'Women can be dangerous, sometimes. Especially to each other.'
That night, Jerry confessed to his wife. 'Who was it?' she shrieked. 'I bet it was that hussy, Amelia.'
'I can't tell you,' said Jerry.
'Oh, I know who it must be. That harlot, what's her name? Amber. She'll sleep with anyone!'
'Look, I can't tell you,' repeated Jerry.
'I know, I know, it's Talia. She's such a tart.'
Once again, Jerry said nothing, and his wife eventually gave up. The next day Jerry met his

Blokes and Chicks

mate down at the pub.
'Hey, Jerry, how did confession time go?'
'Great,' said Jerry. 'Not only did my wife forgive me, she's given me three new leads!'

★ ★ ★

A woman went into a Catholic church and asked the priest if he'd preside over her wedding. 'But I must tell you, Father,' she said, 'that although I have been married three times already, I am still a virgin.'
'I don't see how you could have been married three times and still be a virgin,' said the priest incredulously.
'Well, my first husband was a gynaecologist and all he wanted to do was look at it. My second husband was a psychiatrist and all he wanted to do was talk about it. And my third husband was a carpenter and he always put it off until another day. But the man I want to marry now, Father, is a solicitor, so I know I'm going to get screwed for sure.'

★ ★ ★

Thoroughly pissed off at their lecturer's sexual innuendo, a group of girls decided that the next time he said something inappropriate they would all, en masse, get up and leave the lecture hall. But unbeknownst to them, a male student overheard their plan and filled the lecturer in on it.

The next day, during class, the lecturer suddenly leered, 'You know, I hear there's a shortage of whores in Wellington...'

Exchanging looks, the girls all stood up and started to leave the room.

Looking after them, the lecturer said innocently, 'Girls, girls, where are you going? The next plane to Wellington doesn't leave for two hours!'

★ ★ ★

A rich guy and a poor guy were talking about what they were getting their wives for Christmas. The rich guy said, 'I'm getting Anastasia a fur coat and a BMW. If she doesn't like the coat, she can return it to the store in the car.'

'Wow,' said the poor guy. 'She'll love those gifts. I've got my wife a silk blouse and a vibrator.'

'A vibrator!' exclaimed the rich guy.

'Yep,' replied the poor guy. 'That way, if she doesn't like the blouse she can go @#$% herself.'

★ ★ ★

Blokes and Chicks

A blonde walks into a library. 'Excuse me, can I have a burger and large fries, please?' she asks.
The librarian looks up and shakes her head, chiding, 'Miss, this is a library!'
The blonde then leans over the counter, 'Oh, I'm so sorry!' she whispers, 'Can I have a burger and large fries, please?'

★ ★ ★

A couple went to see their dentist. The man made it clear they were in a very big hurry. 'Don't worry about any of those fancy needles or laughing gas or anything,' he says. Just yank the tooth out and get it over with.'
The dentist said, 'Well, I'm impressed. I wish more people were as brave as you. Which tooth is it?'
The man turned to his wife and said, 'Show him, dear.'

★ ★ ★

Why do you see so many guys hanging out in bars?
They don't have a wife to go home to.
Or they do.

★ ★ ★

A rather inexperienced young man scored a date with the girl of his dreams. Wanting to impress her, he decided to take her out to a really expensive French restaurant in Nelson. Alas, he couldn't read a word of French, but rather than admit this to her, he went ahead and selected a dish for himself.

The waiter sniggered when he ordered his meal, but brought it nevertheless, a whole pig - including the head - smothered in barbecue sauce. When the waiter wheeled it over, the poor young man was mortified, but he didn't bat an eyelid. Reaching into the pig's mouth, he took out the red apple.

'I know it's extravagant,' he told his date, 'but this is the only way I like fruit.'

★ ★ ★

'Minister,' the secretary called out across the office, 'there's a woman here on the phone who wants to know what you plan to do about the abortion bill.'

Immediately going bright red, the minister spluttered, 'Er, tell her I'll have a cheque in the mail by morning.'

★ ★ ★

Blokes and Chicks

Why do they call it PMS?
Mad Cow Disease was already taken.

★ ★ ★

A woman, who was trying to interest her husband in a bit of 'action', went to the lounge room where he was watching TV and said, 'Honey, today I went to the doctor for my annual check-up. He had me take off all

my clothes and then told me I had the most beautiful breasts and legs he'd ever seen.'
'Oh yeah?' sneered her husband. 'What did he say about your fat arse?'
'To be honest, darling,' she replied, 'your name was never mentioned.'

★ ★ ★

I stopped at a friend's house the other day and found him stalking around with a fly-swatter. When I asked if he had gotten any flies, he answered, 'Yeah, three males and two females.'
Curious, I asked how he could tell the difference. He answered, 'Three were on a beer can and two were on the phone.'

★ ★ ★

Blokes and Chicks

What do 'light' and 'hard' have in common?
You can't sleep with a light on, either.

★ ★ ★

A man walks into a bank and screams, 'This is a f*$# up!'
The teller replies, 'Don't you mean "this is a hold up"?'
'Nope, it's most definitely a f*$# up,' the robber replies. 'I forgot my gun.'

★ ★ ★

Two drunks staggered past a bus depot. 'Hey, let's steal a bus so we can drive home,' slurred one drunk.

The other drunk peered bleary-eyed through the mesh fence, 'Don't bother,' he mumbled to his mate, 'the number 39 to Henderson is right down the back. We'll never get it out.'

★ ★ ★

On an archaeological dig one day in Rotorua, an archaeologist found a tablet with symbols carved in it, thought to be over two thousand years old. Excited, the archaeologist called a press conference to tell the world of his find.

'We can infer a great many things about the society that carved these symbols,' he began. 'The presence of the cross indicates that Christianity was introduced in New Zealand long, long ago. The presence of a shovel indicates that even that long ago, New Zealanders were builders. This third symbol here, which looks rather like a donkey, suggests they had domesticated animals, and this fourth picture, a baby fowl, shows us that they were farmers.'

'Crap!' yelled out a man from the audience. 'Anyone with half a brain knows that it's really early Kiwi pornography.'

'Oh?' said the discoverer of the symbols, 'And

why do you say that?'
'Because,' he replied, 'what it really says is, "Jesus, dig the arse on that chick!".'

★ ★ ★

What is twelve inches long and white?
Nothing.

★ ★ ★

Tony walks into his doctor's rooms when all of a sudden a nun runs past him screaming. When he is called in for his consultation, Tony asks, 'So what's up with the nun, doc? She was tearing through the surgery like it was the end of the world!'
'Well, I just told her that she's pregnant,' the doctor explains.
'You've got to be joking!' exclaims Tony, 'A pregnant nun!'
'No, no,' replies the doctor. 'She's not pregnant. But I sure as Hell cured her hiccups!'

★ ★ ★

How do you make a hormone?
Don't pay her.

★ ★ ★

One day Mr Arcadie drove with his wife to the kindergarten they had both attended as youngsters. They stood outside the gate and pointed at the playground they used to play in, and the big oak tree where they had carved their initials inside a heart. They smiled at each other, remembering their blossoming love.

As they drove home, the Arcadies found themselves behind an armoured van and when it hit a bump, a sack of money fell out. The Arcadies quickly picked up the sack and found that it contained one million dollars. Honest Mr Arcadie said to his wife, 'Well, Bessie, we'll have to give it back!'

She looked at him incredulously, saying, 'Like Hell we will!' and they drove home in stony silence.

The next day, two policemen came to their door. 'We're asking everyone in the neighbourhood if they've come across a bag with money in it,' said one of the cops.

'No,' said Bessie.

'Yes,' said her husband.

Bessie glared at him, then turned to the cops, 'You'll have to excuse my husband. He's got Alzheimer's.'

'No, I have not!' Mr Arcadie answered indignantly. 'Bessie and I were driving home from kindergarten and...'

Blokes and Chicks

'Come on,' said the cop rolling his eyes at his associate. 'Let's move on to the next house.'

★ ★ ★

What's the similarity between marriage and a tornado?
At first there's a lot of blowing and sucking, then boom! Your house is gone.

★ ★ ★

A lady was enjoying a stroll in the park with her poodle when it is suddenly mounted by a rottweiler. The large mutt is really humping away, and despite the lady's frantic efforts, she's unable to split them apart.
The young boy who owns the rottweiler walks up to the copulating beasts and carefully sticks his finger up the rottweiler's rear-end.
Suddenly, the action stops.
The lady is amazed, 'How did you do that, young man?'
The boy replies, 'Well, old Rusty here can certainly dish it out, but he definitely cannot take it!'

★ ★ ★

More Great Kiwi Jokes

A middle-aged couple go to the A&P show at Mystery Creek and end up at the cattle auction. They notice signs taped to the backs of three bulls. The first sign said: 'This bull mated fifty times last year!'
The wife turned to her husband and scoffs, 'Fifty times! You could learn a thing or two from this bull, dear!'
The next bull's sign stated: 'This bull mated sixty-five times last year!'
Again, the wife turned to her husband and sneers, 'Sixty-five times! You could certainly learn a thing or two from this beast!'
They proceeded to the third bull and his sign read: 'This bull mated 365 times last year!'
The wife's mouth drops to the ground and she says, 'My Lord! That's once a day. You REALLY could learn a thing or two from this bull!'
The husband, silent until now, suddenly turns to his wife and snaps, 'I bet he didn't have to do it 365 times with the same blimmin' cow!'

★ ★ ★

A man took a lady out to dinner for the first time. The meal was wonderful, the ambience romantic. Later they went on to the theatre and saw a fantastic play. The evening was a huge success, and as he dropped her at her door he said, 'I have had a lovely time. You

Blokes and Chicks

looked so glorious, you remind me of a beautiful rambling rose. May I see you tomorrow?' She agreed and a date was made. The next night, holding a big box of chocolates, he knocked on her door. When the woman opened it, she slapped him hard across the face. He was stunned.
'What was that for?' he asked.
She said, 'I looked up "rambling rose" in the encyclopaedia last night and it said, "Not well suited to bedding, but is excellent for rooting up against a garden wall.".'

★ ★ ★

A man rushes into his house and yells at his wife, 'Marama! Pack your things. I've just won lotto!'
Marama shrieks, 'My God, really?! Shall I pack for warm weather or for cold?'
'I don't care,' says her husband. 'Just so long as you bugger off before lunch time!'

★ ★ ★

In the beginning, God created Earth and rested.
Then God created man and rested.
Then God created woman.
Since then, neither God nor man has rested.

★ ★ ★

More Great Kiwi Jokes

A man walked into a cafe and said to the waitress, 'My name is Brodie, and I have a proposition for you. I'll bet ten thousand dollars to your one hundred dollars that by this time tomorrow your nipples will have disappeared.'

The waitress was shocked, but her wages were pretty pathetic, so she thought she'd give it a go. 'Okay, you're on,' she said.

The two shook hands, and the man left, promising to meet her the next day.

For the rest of the day, the waitress was ultra paranoid about her breasts. She bandaged them up to protect them. She kept away from all sharp objects. She even had a cold shower just to ensure that she wouldn't burn her nipples.

The next day, Brodie returned to the cafe where the waitress worked, this time accompanied by a businessman. Brodie walked up to the waitress and said, 'Well?' With a triumphant expression, the waitress tore open her blouse and flashed her boobs at Brodie and the businessman. The nipples were still there, normal as ever.

The businessman gasped and fell to the floor. Brodie handed the waitress ten thousand dollars, then bent down and reached into the businessman's pocket.

'What's the story?' asked the waitress,

Blokes and Chicks

gesturing to the businessman.
'Easy,' said Brodie. 'I bet him fifty thousand dollars that I could walk in here and have you flash your boobs at me.'

★ ★ ★

A journalist had won the privilege of being the only one in all of New Zealand to be granted an interview with Neil Armstrong, the first man to walk on the moon. At the start of the interview, while she was setting up her tape recorder, she said, 'Mr Armstrong, before we get going with my questions, I'd like to say that I was only ten years old when I watched you land on the moon. I was so in awe of you, and when you said the words "One small step for man, one giant step for mankind" I felt my heart go thump and I have never forgotten that moment. It really meant a lot to me and to everyone else who heard it.'

Neil Armstrong replied, 'Well, thanks, but errm, uh, that's not exactly what I said.'

'Really?' replied the journo. 'That's odd. Well, what did you say?'

Neil replied, 'What I really said was "One small step for man, one giant step for Mel Kind".

Aghast, the journo replied, 'One giant step for Mel Kind? What on Earth does that mean?'

'Well,' replied Neil, 'my family was very poor when I was growing up. We lived in one of those low-rent, high-rise apartment buildings. Mel Kind and his family lived in the apartment next to ours, and because the walls in those buildings were so thin we could hear everything that went on in the surrounding apartments. Every night I heard exactly what went on in there. Well, one night, very late, I woke up to hear Mel making love to his wife. In the heat of it all, Mel asked his wife for a blow job. She said to him, "Mel, that's

Blokes and Chicks

disgusting! The day I ever give you a blow job will be the day a man walks on the moon!"'

★ ★ ★

Nine out of ten guys prefer women with large breasts. The tenth guy usually prefers the nine other guys.

★ ★ ★

A couple in their seventies make an appointment to see a sex therapist. Once in the consultation room, they ask the therapist if he'll watch them having sex. Perplexed, the doctor agrees and sits quietly while the couple hop to it.
After a screaming climax, the therapist offers his opinion, 'There's nothing wrong with you two at all. And I'm a bit embarrassed to charge you, but here's my bill.'
Unperturbed, the couple pay the $100 fee and leave, only to return the next week and repeat the exercise.
This continues on for several weeks and the therapist has to conclude that no matter what position, these pensioners are perfectly adequate at rooting.
Finally, he asks them, 'What exactly are you trying to find out? You have a healthier sex life

than I do, and it costs you $100 to visit me each week.'

The old bloke says, 'She's married, so we can't go to her house. And I'm married, so we can't go to mine.'

'But why come to me?' retorts the therapist.

'Well, the Hilton charges $300, the Novotel $200, and here we can do it for just $100. Not only that, but I get $80 back on my medical insurance.'

★ ★ ★

A group of girlfriends went on a long-awaited holiday by the beach. They saw a groovy-looking five-storey hotel with a sign on the front door that read: 'For Women Only', and they thought they'd try it out. They went inside and the bouncer, a very handsome guy with bulging muscles and well-tanned skin, greeted them and explained to them how the hotel worked.

'We have five floors,' he began. 'Go up floor by floor, and once you find what you are looking for, you can stay there. Each floor has a sign telling you what's inside, so you won't find it hard to decide where you want to stay the night.'

So the women start going up, and on the first floor the sign read: 'All the men here are

Blokes and Chicks

horrible lovers, but they are sensitive and kind.' The friends laughed and without hesitation went up to the next floor. The sign on the second floor read: 'All the men here are wonderful lovers, but they generally treat women badly.' This wasn't going to do, so the friends moved up to the third floor where the sign read: 'All the men here are great lovers and sensitive to the needs of women.' This was good, but there were still two more floors. So on the group went to the fourth floor, where the sign was perfect: 'All the men here have perfect builds; are sensitive and attentive to women; are perfect lovers; they are also single, rich and straight.' The women seemed pleased, but they decide that they would rather see what the fifth floor had to offer before settling on the fourth. When they reached the fifth floor, there was only a sign that read: 'There are no men here. This floor was built only to prove that there is no way to please a woman.'

★ ★ ★

More Great Kiwi Jokes

Why It's Better Being a Male
1. Your orgasms are real. Always.
2. Your last name stays put.
3. The garage is all yours.
4. Wedding plans take care of themselves.
5. Car mechanics tell you the truth.
6. You don't care if someone doesn't notice your new haircut.
7. No one gives you disapproving looks if you have leg hair stubble.
8. Wrinkles add character.
9. One-night stands are an expected occurrence.
10. People never glance at your chest when you're talking to them.
11. The occasional well-rendered belch is practically expected.
12. New shoes don't cut, blister, or mangle your feet.
13. Porn movies are designed with you in mind.
14. Not liking a person does not preclude having great sex with them.
15. Your pals can be trusted never to trap you with: 'So, notice anything different?'
16. You can appreciate great sport.
17. You can throw a ball more than two metres.
18. A week's holiday requires only one suitcase.

Blokes and Chicks

19. You can open all your own jars.
20. Drycleaners and hairdressers don't rob you blind.
21. You can go to a public toilet without a support group.
22. You don't have to clean up the house before the cleaner arrives.
23. You get extra credit for the slightest act of thoughtfulness.
24. If someone forgets to invite you to something, he or she can still be your friend.
25. If you are 31 and single, nobody whispers about you and shakes their head.
26. You don't have to clean your flat if the electricity meter reader is coming.

27. You can sit in silence watching a football game with your mate for hours without ever thinking 'He must be mad at me.'

More Great Kiwi Jokes

28. You can drop by to see a friend without having to bring morning tea.
29. If another guy shows up at the party in the same outfit, you just might become lifelong friends.
30. You don't have to stop and think which way to turn a nut on a bolt.
31. Wrinkles in clothes are invisible to you.
32. The same hairstyle lasts for years, maybe decades.
33. You don't have to buy toilet paper at every shopping trip.
34. Everything you might possibly need within the course of the day can fit in your back jeans pocket.
35. You can 'do' your nails with a bread knife.

★ ★ ★

A cowboy and his bride ask the hotel desk clerk for a room, telling him that they just got married.
'Congratulations!' exclaims the clerk, 'Luckily, all of our suites are free tonight. Would you like the bridal?'
'No, thanks,' says the cowboy, 'I'll just hold her by the ears til she gets the hang of it.'

★ ★ ★

Blokes and Chicks

Father O'Brien was greeting his parishioners one Sunday morning when Mary came running up to him in tears.
'What's bothering you, dear?' he asked.
'My husband's just passed away, Father,' she replied.
'Oh Mary,' said the Father, 'that's terrible. Tell me, did he have any last requests?'
'Why, yes he did, Father,' replied Mary. 'He said, "Please, Mary, put down the gun.".'

★ ★ ★

Walking down the main street of Gore, a woman notices a shop she'd never seen before. Pinned to the front door is a sign: 'Frog with twelve-inch tongue inside. Gives ladies "special attention".'
Intrigued, the woman quickly slips inside the store. However, the shop is almost bare.
'Excuse me, can you help me?' she asks the man behind the counter.
He looks up and grins mischievously, 'Oui, mademoiselle!'

★ ★ ★

An old codger dies and finds himself at the gates of Hell. The Devil suddenly appears and shouts, 'Cower, mere mortal! I am the Devil,

More Great Kiwi Jokes

Lord of Darkness!'
The old bloke just says, 'Uh-huh.'
The Devil is astounded, so he bellows, 'Grovel you little worm! I am Lucifer, Prince of Night and Master of Evil! Your soul is mine!'
The old man simply shrugs and says, 'Yep.'
The Devil is infuriated. 'Why do you not shake with terror? Why do you not quake in fear?'
'Mate,' comes the old bloke's reply, 'I've been married to your sister for 50-odd years!'

★ ★ ★

Blokes and Chicks

A man walking along a street in Auckland was deep in prayer. All of a sudden he said out loud, 'Lord, grant me one wish.'
Suddenly the sky clouded above his head and in a booming voice the Lord said, 'Because you have been faithful to me in all ways, I will grant you one wish.'
The man said, 'Build a bridge to Australia so I can drive over for business any time I want.'
The Lord said, 'Your request is very grandiose and lacking thought. Think of the logistics of that kind of undertaking. The length of the supports required to reach the bottom of the ocean! The strength and durability they would have to possess! The concrete and steel it would take! I can do it, but it is extremely hard for me to justify your desire for worldly things. Take a little more time and think of another wish, a wish that is a little more reasonable.'
The man thought about it for a long time. He took days and nights pondering what he could wish for. Finally he said, 'Lord, I have been married and divorced four times. All of my wives said that I am uncaring and insensitive. I wish that I could understand women. I want to know how they feel inside, what they are thinking when they give me the silent treatment, why they cry, what they mean when they say "nothing's wrong" and how I

can make a woman truly happy.'
God thought gravely for a few minutes and then said, 'You want two lanes or four on that bridge?'

★ ★ ★

A couple honeymooning in an old hotel had gone up to their room on arrival and hadn't been seen since. After two days, the manager knocked on their door and asked if they were all right.
'Yes, thanks,' came the reply.
'Do you want any food?' asked the manager.
'No, we are living on the fruits of love.'
'Okay,' said the manager, 'but would you stop throwing the skins out the window because they're choking my ducks.'

★ ★ ★

How do you fix a woman's watch?
You don't. There is a clock on the oven.

★ ★ ★

A secretary answers the phone in a busy office, 'Good morning, Masterson Parachute Club.'
There is a sharp intake of breath on the other

Blokes and Chicks

end of the line, 'Excuse me,' says a man, 'but don't you mean the "Masterson Prostitute's Club"?'
'Oh, no, sir!' laughs the secretary, 'This is definitely a parachute club!'
'Bugger,' replies the man. 'Yesterday your salesman called and signed me up for two jumps a week.'

★ ★ ★

Why do women have smaller feet than men? It's one of those 'evolutionary things' that allows them to stand closer to the kitchen sink.

★ ★ ★

A beggar walked up to a model and said, 'Please, lady, can I have some spare change? I haven't eaten for days.'
She replied, 'God, I wish I had your willpower.'

★ ★ ★

Young son: 'Is it true, Dad? I heard that in some parts of Africa a man doesn't know his wife until he marries her.'
Dad: 'That happens in every country, son.'

★ ★ ★

More Great Kiwi Jokes

Thor, the God of thunder, came down to spend a day with mere mortals and thought he'd like a bit of nooky whilst in his human state. Well, he let sparks fly with a young lady who had a slight speech impediment. When it was time to depart back to the Heavens, for his leave pass was up, his guilty conscience got to him and he thought he'd better tell the young lady who he was. 'I'm Thor,' he said. 'Tho am I,' lisped the girl, 'but I'm thatithfied.'

★ ★ ★

It was the eve of Tom's wedding, so his father sat him down for a man-to-man chat. 'Now, lad,' said the father, 'let me tell you something. On my wedding night in our honeymoon suite, I took off my trousers and handed them to your mother, and said, "Here, honey, try

Blokes and Chicks

these on." So, she did and she said, "Well, dear, they're a little too big; I can't wear them." So I replied, "Exactly. I wear the trousers in this family and I always will." Ever since that night we have been right as rain.'
'Thanks for the tip,' said Tom.
On the night of the wedding, Tom took off his trousers and said to his new wife Salli, 'Here, babe, try these on.'
She obliged, and said, 'Thanks, Tom, but these are a bit too big; they don't fit me.'
So Tom replied, 'Exactly. I wear the trousers in this family and I always will, and I don't want you to ever forget that.'
Then Salli took off her undies, passed them to Tom and said, 'Here, you try on mine.' So he did and said, 'I can't even get into your knickers.'
Salli replied, 'Exactly. And if you don't change your bloody attitude, you never will.'

★ ★ ★

A woman is widowed and sick of being alone. She puts an ad in a newspaper saying, 'Woman seeking a man who is good in bed, won't abuse her, and won't run away.' Months pass and one day her doorbell rings. She opens the door, and a man with no legs and no arms is in a wheelchair on her porch.

She asks, 'Can I help you?'
The man says, 'I came in to answer your advert. I am your perfect man.'
She says, 'What makes you think that?'
He answers, 'I have no arms so I can't abuse you, and I have no legs so I can't run away.'
The woman says, 'Yeah, but how do I know that you are good in bed?'
He smirks proudly, 'Well, how do you think I rang the doorbell?'

★ ★ ★

If Men Wrote for Women's Magazines

Q: My husband wants to experience three-in-a-bed-sex with me and my sister. What should I do?

A: *Your husband is clearly devoted to you. He can't get enough of you, so he goes for the next best thing: your sister. Far from being an issue, this will bring the family together. Why not get some cousins involved? If you are still unsure, then let him sleep with your sister, just the two of them, and while he's doing that, you go out and buy him an expensive present, and cook him a nice meal.*

Q: My husband continually asks me to perform oral sex with him.

Blokes and Chicks

A: *Do it. Sperm is not only delicious, but it has only 15 kilojoules per teaspoon. Men know that sperm gives you a healthy glow, so they are really just trying to do you a favour by letting you perform oral sex on them. The best thing to do is to thank him, buy him an expensive present, and cook him a nice meal.*

Q: My husband has too many nights out with the boys down at the pub.
A: *This is perfectly natural behaviour – encourage him. If he is going out just once a week it is certainly not enough – three nights should be the minimum. The man is a hunter and he needs to prove his courage to his friends. A night out with the boys is a stressful affair, and to get back to you is a relief. Just look back at how emotional and happy and relaxed the man is when he returns home to you. The best thing to do is to buy him an expensive present, and cook him a nice meal.*

Q: My husband doesn't know where my clitoris is.
A: *Your clitoris is of no concern to your husband. If you must mess with it do it in your own time. To help with the family budget you may wish to video tape yourself*

while doing this, and to sell it at flea markets. To ease your selfish guilt, buy your man an expensive present, and cook him a nice meal.

Q: My husband is uninterested in foreplay.
A: *Foreplay to a man is very hurtful. What it means is that you do not love your man as much as you should – you should get in the mood without any effort on his part.*
Abandon all wishes in this area, and make it up to him by buying a nice expensive present, and cooking a nice meal.

Q: My husband has never given me an orgasm.
A: *The female orgasm is a myth. It is fostered by militant, man-hating feminists and is a danger to the family unit. Don't mention it again to him and show your love to him by buying a nice expensive present, and cook him a nice meal.*

Q: How do I know if I'm ready for sex?
A: *Ask your boyfriend. He'll know when the time is right. When it comes to love and sex, men are much more responsible, since they're not as confused emotionally as women. It's a proven fact.*

Blokes and Chicks

Q: Should I have sex on the first date?
A: *Yes. Beforehand, if possible.*

Q: What exactly happens during the act of sex?
A: *Again, this is entirely up to the man. The important thing to remember is that you must do whatever he tells you without question. Sometimes, he'll even ask you to do certain things that may seem slightly perverted to you. Do them anyway.*

Q: What is 'afterplay?'
A: *After a man has finished making love, he needs to replenish his manly energy. 'Afterplay' is simply a list of important activities for you to do after the lovemaking. This includes lighting his cigarette, making him pizza, bringing him a few beers, or leaving him alone to sleep while you go out and buy him an expensive gift.*

Q: Does the size of the penis matter?
A: *Yes. Although many women believe that quality, not quantity, is important, studies show this is simply not true. The average erect male penis measures about three inches. Anything longer than that is extremely rare and, if by some chance your lover's sexual organ is four inches or over, you should go down on your knees and*

thank your lucky stars you have been given such a fine lover. Do everything possible to please him, such as doing his laundry, cleaning his home and buying him an expensive gift.

★ ★ ★

Two friends were sitting in a bar drowning their sorrows.
'I was in my fifteen-year-old daughter's room this morning,' said the first man, 'and I found a packet of contraceptive pills. I didn't even know she was having sex!'
'Really?' says the second man, 'Well, I was in my daughter's room this morning and found a box of condoms. And I didn't even know that she had a penis!'

★ ★ ★

On a farm not too far from Palmerston North lived a chicken and a horse, who spent every day playing together. One day, the two were playing when the horse fell into a bog and began to sink. Scared for his life, the horse whinnied for the chicken to go get the farmer for help. Off the chicken ran, back to the

Blokes and Chicks

farm, clucking frantically all the way.
Arriving at the farm, he searched and searched for the farmer, but to no avail, for he had gone to town with the only tractor. Running around, the chicken spied the farmer's new BMW. (Yes, some farmers do manage to make a good living.) The chicken found the keys, picked up a rope and drove back to the bog where the horse was still struggling for its life. The horse was surprised, but happy, to see the chicken arrive in the shiny BMW, and he managed to get a hold of the loop of rope the chicken tossed to him. After tying the other end to the rear bumper of the farmer's car, the chicken then drove slowly forward and, with the aid of the powerful car, rescued the horse! Happy and proud, the chicken drove the BMW back to the farmhouse, and the farmer was none the wiser when he returned.
A few weeks later, after some heavy rain, it was the chicken's turn to fall into the bog, and soon, he too, began to sink.
'Help, horse, help!' he clucked in panic. The horse thought a moment, walked over, and straddled the large bog. Looking underneath, he told the chicken to grab his 'thing' and he would then lift him out. The chicken got a good grip, and the horse pulled him up and out, saving his life.
The moral of the story? When you're hung like

a horse, you don't need a BMW to pick up chicks.

★ ★ ★

A man and his wife were having some problems at home and were giving each other the silent treatment. The next week the man realised that he would need his wife to wake him at 5 a.m. for an early flight to Christchurch. Not wanting to be the first to break the silence, he finally wrote on a piece of paper, 'Please wake me at 5 a.m.'
The next morning, the man woke up only to discover it was 9 a.m., and that he had missed his flight. Furious, he was about to go and see why his wife hadn't woken him when he noticed a piece of paper by the bed. It said, 'It's 5 a.m., wake up!'

★ ★ ★

A man was reading the paper when he saw an advertisement saying, 'Porsche for sale! Brand new, only $100.' The guy thought there must have been a misprint, but he thought, 'Well, why not, what have I got to lose?' So he went to the address and met the lady who was selling the car.
After talking to her for a while he learnt that

yes, the Porsche was brand new, and it really was only $100.
'I'll take it!' he said. 'But why are you selling me this great Porsche for only $100?' The lady replied with a bitter laugh. 'My husband just ran off with his secretary, and he told me, "You can have the house and the furniture, but sell my Porsche and send me the money".'

★ ★ ★

A man and woman were having drinks when they got into an argument about who enjoyed sex more. The man said, 'Men definitely enjoy sex more than women. Why else do you think we spend 98 per cent of our time thinking about it?'
'That doesn't prove anything,' countered the woman. 'An analogy: when your ear itches and you put your little finger in and wriggle it around, which feels better, your ear or your finger?'

★ ★ ★

The Pope Walked Into a Bar One Day...

Two Jewish guys were seated together on the flight from Wellington to Auckland. They'd been in the air for about half an hour when the younger man asked the other if he had the time. There was no answer.

So he tried again. 'Can you tell me the time please?' But again there was no answer.

It wasn't until the aeroplane was descending that the old man quickly looked at his watch and said it was four-thirty.

The young man asked, perplexed, 'Well, why on Earth didn't you tell me the time earlier?'

'Well, you know what it is like,' began the man, 'people get talking to each other in situations like these. We could become friends, especially as we are both Jewish. I'd be obliged to invite you home for dinner. I have a lovely daughter and you are a young,

The Pope Walked Into a Bar One Day...

handsome man. Romance could blossom and before long you could be asking for her hand in marriage. And, to put it bluntly, I don't want no son-in-law who hasn't got a watch.'

★ ★ ★

A young boy was having problems learning maths at school, so his parents decided to send him to a private Catholic college, hoping that the schooling there would be better. Well, what do you know, after a semester in the new school the boy was getting straight As in all his subjects - even in maths!
Surprised, his mother said, 'You must really love it there to be doing so well!'
'Not really,' said the boy. 'It's just that as soon as I saw that guy nailed to the plus sign, I knew they meant business!'

★ ★ ★

Why did God invent alcohol?
So ugly people could have sex.

★ ★ ★

A drunk stumbles upon a Baptism service one Sunday afternoon down by the river. The minister turns and sees him and says, 'Mister,

are you ready to find Jesus?'
The drunk looks around him and says, 'Yes, sir, I am!'
The minister then dunks the fellow under the water and pulls him right back up. 'Have you found Jesus?' the minister asks.
'No, I have not!' says the drunk.
The minister dunks him again, brings him up and says, 'Now, brother, have you found Jesus?'
'No, I have not!' says the drunk again.
Rolling his eyes, the minister holds the man under the water for quite a long time, brings him up and demands, 'For the love of God, have you found Jesus yet?'
The old drunk wipes his eyes and pleads, 'Are you sure this is where he fell in?'

★ ★ ★

The elder priest, speaking to the younger priest, said, 'Brother, I need to discuss something with you. Now, I know you were reaching out to the young people when you put comfortable recliners in to replace the first four pews. It worked. We got the front of the church filled first; that was a good plan.'
The younger priest smiled, 'Why, thank you, Father!'
The elder one continued, 'And, you told me a

The Pope Walked Into a Bar One Day...

little more beat to the music would bring young people back to church, so I supported you when you brought in that rock and roll gospel choir that packed us to the balcony.'
'So,' said the younger priest, 'what's the problem then?'
'Well,' said the elder priest, 'I'm afraid you've gone too far with the drive-thru confessional.'
'But Father,' protested the younger priest. 'My confessions have nearly doubled since I began that!'
'I know, my son, but the flashing "Toot 'n Tell or Go to Hell" neon pink sign really has to go.'

★ ★ ★

A man rushed into the confessional and blurted, 'Father, I had sex with a pair of stunning eighteen-year-old nymphomaniacs five times last week!'
'My goodness! What kind of Catholic are you?' roared the priest.
'I'm not a bloody Catholic,' the man snorted.
'Then why are you telling me this?' said the priest, perplexed.
'Mate, I'm telling EVERYONE!'

★ ★ ★

Jesus was taking a wander through Heaven when he notices an old man sitting on a doorstep, looking rather sadly at his shoes. 'Mate,' says Jesus, 'you're in Heaven, you should be happy! What's the problem?'
The old man continues to look down at his shoes and sighs, 'I've been looking for my son and I haven't been able to find him.'
Jesus says kindly, 'Tell me about it.'
'Well,' begins the man, 'on Earth I was a carpenter, and one day my son just disappeared. I never heard from him again, and I was hoping to find him here in Heaven.'
With his heart suddenly beating faster, Jesus bent over the old man and said, 'Father?'
The old man turned, looked up and cried, 'Pinocchio?'

★ ★ ★

Before they could be ordained, the three young men had to be tested to determine if they were really as chaste as they should be for the role they were to assume. A priest ordered them to strip. Once the young men did this, he attached rubber bands to their private parts and ushered them into a bedroom where a gorgeous naked girl lay on the bed.
After a few minutes one of the students got a bit excited and '*boing!*' – out he popped. He

was promptly and sternly told to head to the showers to settle himself down. A moment later it happened to one of the remaining students – '*boing!* He, too, was sent to the showers. Minutes passed, and when the third student still looked calm and composed, the priest congratulated him and said, 'Well done, my son, now join the other two in the showers.'
'*Boing!*'

★ ★ ★

Kneeling unsteadily on the floor, an old black preacher, who was dying, took his Bible and prayed to God. 'Almighty God,' he said, 'I have been your faithful servant all my life. I am now almost on my deathbed, and I ask you, nay I beg you, just to answer me one question. Lord, are you black or are you white?'
Suddenly, the room darkened, a flash of light burst into the room, and a voice boomed out, 'I am what I am.'
The preacher's brow knotted. 'Please, Lord, that's no answer. I need to know!'
The voice boomed again, 'Dummy! If I were black I would have said unto Moses and now unto you, "I be what I be, man!".'

★ ★ ★

Moses came down from the mountain one day with two large stone tablets and met his friend Abraham. 'Well, Moses,' said Abraham, 'I see you've brought God's commandments with you. What's the news?'
'Well, Abraham,' said Moses. 'It didn't go too badly. I've got good news and bad news.'
'Give me the good news first,' Abraham said.
'Well, the good news is, I talked Him down from fifteen commandments to only ten.'
'You beauty! So, what's the bad news?'
Moses sighed, 'The bad news is adultery is still in.'

★ ★ ★

The Pope Walked Into a Bar One Day...

The president of McDonalds was in Rome for a meeting with the Pope. He said to the Pope, 'Your Holiness, my company has a lucrative proposition for the church. We will pay the church one billion dollars if you agree to change the words of "give us this day our daily bread" to "give us this day our daily Big Mac".'

The Holy Father answered that under no circumstances would the church consider such a thing.

The president of McDonalds replied, 'Your Holiness, that is just our first offer. We are prepared to pay you two billion dollars if you will change the words in the Lord's prayer from "give us this day our daily bread" to "give us this day our daily Big Mac".'

The Holy Father again replied that the traditions of the Catholic Church were not measured in financial terms and that the offer must be refused.

The president then went back to his hotel, but the next day he returned to see the Pope one more time. 'Your Holiness, I have discussed our offer with my board of directors. They asked me to come by one more time with a final offer to see if we can get you to change the words in the Lord's prayer from "give us this day our daily bread" to "give us this day our daily Big Mac". If your church will agree

to this, my company is prepared to offer you ten billion dollars.'
The Pope turned to one of the cardinals beside him and said, 'Cardinal, exactly when does our contract with that bakery expire?'

★ ★ ★

What do you get when you cross a nun with a PC?
A computer that will never go down on you.

★ ★ ★

A young pastor, who normally rode a bike, was walking gloomily down the street when he came upon an older pastor. The older pastor could see his young friend was troubled deeply.
'What is bothering you, my son?' he asked.
'Well, it appears a member of my congregation has stolen my bike,' he replied sadly. The elder said, 'If I may give you some advice you might get your bike back. Next Sunday morning during your sermon, preach about the Ten Commandments, and when you get to "Thou shall not steal" really emphasise it.'
Well, the next week the two pastors met again, and this time the young pastor was riding his bike.

The Pope Walked Into a Bar One Day...

'Well,' said the older one, 'I see my advice worked.'
'Yes,' the young one replied, 'I took your advice and preached on the Ten Commandments. When I got to "Though shall not commit adultery" I remembered where I left my bike.'

★ ★ ★

Jesus walks into a hotel, tosses some nails on the reception desk and says, 'Can you put me up for the night?'

★ ★ ★

Two clergymen were attending a special cruise together one day. Suddenly, in the middle of a theological panel discussion attended by several well-known and respected New Zealand church leaders, the ship sprung a leak and began to sink. One of the clergymen said, 'Let's help get the women to the lifeboats!'
Running toward a lifeboat, the other one yelled, 'Screw the women!'
Taking a quick look at the rising water above them, the first one asked, 'Do you think there's time?'

★ ★ ★

What do you get when you cross a Jehovah's Witness with a Hell's Angel?
Somebody who comes to your door and tells you to @#$% off.

★ ★ ★

Why doesn't Jesus eat M&Ms?
They fall through his hands.

★ ★ ★

Kermit the Frog is sitting at a bar drowning his sorrows.
'Hey Kermit, why are you looking so glum?' asks Fozzie Bear.
'Well, Fozzie, I'm having a real problem with Miss Piggy,' says Kermit, 'she wants me to go down on her, but I simply can't do it.'
'Why not?' asks Fozzie, 'You're not a prude, are you?'
'No. But I am Jewish.'

★ ★ ★

A man came back to bed and proclaimed that he'd just witnessed a miracle.
'You see, when I went to the bathroom the light went on all by itself. Then when I'd finished my business, the light went off all by

The Pope Walked Into a Bar One Day...

itself,' he explained to his wife.
'That's no miracle,' scoffed his missus, 'you're bloody drunk and you've pissed in the fridge again!'

★ ★ ★

Why does the Pope wear his underpants in the bath?
It upsets him to see the unemployed.

★ ★ ★

One day, a rather randy gay fellow dies in a car accident and goes to Heaven. At the pearly gates Saint Peter is waiting for him. After reviewing his records, Saint Peter decides to let him in. 'Follow me,' he says, opening the gate and walking in.
After a hundred metres or so, Saint Peter accidentally drops the keys to the pearly gates and bends over to pick them up. The randy guy, being attracted to Saint Peter, just can't resist, so he jumps on him and does his thing. Saint Peter is furious.
'If you do that again, you'll go straight to Hell! Now just follow me and behave yourself.'
So they continue along, and once more, Peter drops his keys. Once again, the man jumps on him. Saint Peter is now even more furious

than before, but he is a Heavenly creature and decides to give the guy one last chance.
They continue their walk and for the third time Peter drops his keys, so he bends over and picks them up. The guy, having absolutely no self-control, jumps on him. Peter is really pissed off now and sends him straight to Hell.

A few weeks later, Saint Peter goes down to Hell to pick up some chilli chips, but this time something is wrong. It is freezing! There's no fire, no lava and in one corner, he finds the devil lying under a stack of blankets freezing his arse off.

'Why is it so Goddamn cold down here?' Peter asks.

The devil replies, 'Well, ever since you sent that new guy down here, I'm afraid to bend over and pick up the firewood!'

★ ★ ★

'Mum,' said little Tommy, 'does Jesus use our bathroom?'
'Why, no, darling,' replied his mother. 'Why do you ask?'
'Because every day, Dad kicks the door and yells, "Jesus, are you still in there?".'

★ ★ ★

The Pope Walked Into a Bar One Day...

Matt and Jack were best friends and had been all their lives. Both were now in their eighties and one day they made a bargain with each other: whoever died first would try their hardest to come back and tell the other what the afterlife was like.

One month after their pact, Jack passed away. Matt was very sad about losing his friend, and was unable to sleep one night when a voice came in through the open window.

'Matt! Matt!'

Matt's eyes opened wide. 'Oh, my goodness! Jack, is that you?'

'Yessiree,' said Jack. 'And I gotta tell you, the afterlife is wonderful!'

'Tell me all about it!' said Matt eagerly.

'Well, in the morning we eat breakfast, and then we make love. Then we eat lunch and then we make love. Then we eat dinner and afterwards, we make love.'

'Holy shit! That sounds fantastic' bellowed Matt. 'I can't wait to go to Heaven!'

'Heaven?' replied Jack. 'Mate, I'm in your front yard! I came back as a rabbit.'

★ ★ ★

Father McCarthy, a white missionary, had worked for years to bring Christianity to the black natives. In particular, he liked to preach

More Great Kiwi Jokes

the moral dangers of having premarital sex. Thanks to his teachings, none of the village girls were sleeping with the village boys until after they were married.

One day, however, a young wife became pregnant and gave birth to a white baby, which sent shock waves through the community. The chief of the village was enraged and went to see the missionary. 'Father McCarthy,' he said, 'you have taught us the rewards of saving ourselves until marriage, yet here we are seeing a girl giving birth to a white child. Since you are the only white man

in the village, you must be the father!'
Smiling innocently, Father McCarthy put his arm around the chief's shoulder.
'Chief,' he said, 'I'm telling you true, the baby isn't mine; it's an albino.'
He directed the chief's attention to a nearby field where there was one black sheep and a handful of white sheep.
'You see, it's just the way nature works, something that just happens now and then.'
Shifting nervously from foot to foot, the chief (who might just have been an Aussie in disguise) said, 'Say no more, Father McCarthy. I won't tell my people about the girl, if you won't tell them about the sheep.'

★ ★ ★

A lovely young woman went to see her village priest about a problem. Upon seeing the girl, the priest was overcome with lust. As she sat down, he crossed his legs and tried not to be aroused.
'What is the problem, my child?' he managed to utter.
'Well, Father,' she began, 'something happened when I went on a date last night. He was very cute, and… well…'
The girl's voice trailed off, and the priest nodded understandingly.

'My dear, I know this is a rather delicate matter. But did he do this?' And with that he slipped his arm around her waist.
She nodded.
'And this?' he asked, kissing her passionately.
Again, she nodded.
Taking off his clothes, the priest then proceeded to make love to her.
'And... did he do this?' he cried.
The woman nodded.
Finally, the priest finished doing the deed with her and said, 'He really did all that?'
'That,' confirmed the woman, 'and so much more.'
'More?' the priest exclaimed. 'But how could he have done more?'
'Well, he gave me herpes,' she replied.

★ ★ ★

It was the start of the school year and the nun introduced herself to her junior class. She went around to each of her new students, asking them what they wanted to be when they grew up.
'I'm gonna be a doctor,' yelled Dave.
'I'm gonna be a firefighter,' smiled Tamsin.
'I'm gonna be a florist,' mumbled Carrie.
'I'm gonna be a prostitute!' squealed Sasha.
The nun passed out upon hearing Sasha's

The Pope Walked Into a Bar One Day...

desired career, and when she came to she found the children gathered around her, looking at her with concern.
'Sasha, Sasha, wh-wh-what did you say you wanted to be?' spluttered the nun.
'A prostitute,' repeated Sasha.
Sitting up and breathing a sigh of relief, the nun smiled, 'Praise the Lord, child. I thought you said "Protestant".'

★ ★ ★

A sassy blonde is telling a priest a dirty joke about Irishmen.
The priest interrupts, 'Young lady, don't you know that I'm a priest, and Irish as well?!'
'Oh, I'm sorry, Father!' apologies the blonde. 'Do you want me to start again and talk a little slower?'

★ ★ ★

Why do Jewish mothers make great parole officers?
They never let anyone finish a sentence.

★ ★ ★

One of the Pope's senior cardinals is having a shower. Although he is strict about the celibacy rules, he feels a desperate need to masturbate. Just as he climaxes, he notices a photographer taking a picture of his holy seed flying through the air.

'Hang on!' he sputters out the window, 'You cannot publish that picture! You'll destroy the Catholic Church!'

'Mate, this little snap will make me famous and set me up financially for the rest of my life,' retorts the photographer.

The cardinal offers to buy the camera and film, and after much negotiating, agrees to a settlement of three million dollars.

After drying off, the cardinal meets his valet who comments on his great new camera and asks, 'Father, how much did that cost you?'

'Three million bucks,' muttered the cardinal.

'Well, they certainly saw you coming, didn't they?'

★ ★ ★

Eira was horrified when his son broke the news to him that he was going to convert from Judaism to Christianity. He went to see his friend to tell him about it.

'Funny you should mention that,' his friend said, 'my son has just told me that he was converting from Judaism to Christianity. Let's

The Pope Walked Into a Bar One Day...

go together to the rabbi and ask his advice.'
Arriving at the synagogue, they sought out the rabbi and told their story.

'Funny you should mention that,' said the rabbi, 'my son has just announced to me that he's converting from Judaism to Christianity, too. I think there's something funny going on here. Let's go talk to God.'

The rabbi bowed his head and said, 'Lord, all of our sons have forsaken our religion for Christianity. Tell us, please, what we should do?'

There was a rumbling in the Heavens and a deep voice echoed though the synagogue. 'Funny you should mention that.'

★ ★ ★

What do you call a nun walking in her sleep?
A roaming Catholic.

★ ★ ★

A fifty-year-old woman suffers a massive heart attack one evening after a big bowl of greasy nachos, and is taken by ambulance to hospital. While she is being operated on, she has a near-death experience and is actually clinically dead.
She sees God and she asks him, 'Is this it? Is my time here on Earth over?'
God replies, 'No. You have another thirty-eight years left.'
The doctors bring her back to life, and when she recovers from the operation she decides that since she has so long to live, she might as well live it as a beautiful woman. She gets liposuction, breast implants, facial peels, collagen injections - the works.
When she leaves the hospital after the last cosmetic procedure, she crosses the road without looking and is hit by a bus and killed.
Arriving in front of God, she fumes, 'What the Hell is going on? You said I had another thirty-eight years left!'
God replies, 'Doris? Is that you? Sorry, love, I didn't recognise you!'

★ ★ ★

The Pope Walked Into a Bar One Day...

An atheist was spending a quiet day fishing when suddenly his boat is attacked by the Loch Ness monster. The huge ugly beast easily tosses the fisherman and his boat high in the air, and opens its mouth, waiting for the fisherman to fall in. As the man flies through the air in horror, he cries out, 'God! Please help me!'

All of a sudden, the man freezes in mid-air, not falling, not moving.

A voice booms down from the Heavens, 'I thought you did not believe in me. Why, then, do you ask for my help?'

The guy replies, 'God, mate, cut me some slack. Twenty seconds ago, I didn't believe in the Loch Ness monster, either.'

★ ★ ★

It is Friday, and four nuns ask their priest for the weekend off. They argue back and forth for a few minutes. Finally, the priest agrees to let them leave the convent for the weekend. 'However,' he says, 'as soon as you get back Monday morning, I want you to confess to me what you did over the weekend.'

The four nuns agree, and run off. Monday comes, and the four nuns return.

The first nun goes to the priest and says, 'Forgive me, Father, for I have sinned.'

The priest asks, 'What did you do, Sister?'
She replies, 'I watched an R-rated movie.'
The priest looks up at Heaven for a few seconds, then replies, 'You are forgiven. Go and drink the holy water.'
The first nun leaves, and the fourth nun begins to chuckle quietly under her breath.
The second nun then goes up to the priest and says, 'Forgive me, Father, for I have sinned.'
The priest replies, 'Okay, what happened?'
She says, 'I was driving my brother's car down the street in front of his house, and I hit a neighbour's dog and killed it.'
The priest looks up to Heaven for half a minute and says, 'You are forgiven. Go and drink the holy water.'
The second nun goes out. By this time, the fourth nun is laughing quite audibly.
Then the third nun walks up to the priest and says, 'Forgive me, Father, for I have sinned.'
The priest says, 'You - out with it. What did you do?'
She says, 'Last night, I ran naked up and down Queen Street.'
The priest looks up at Heaven for a full five minutes before responding, 'God forgives you. Go and drink the holy water.'
She leaves. The fourth nun falls on the floor, laughing so hard tears run down her cheeks.

The Pope Walked Into a Bar One Day...

The priest asks her, 'Okay. What did you do that was so bloody funny?'
The fourth nun replies, 'I pissed in the holy water.'

★ ★ ★

Short summary of every Jewish holiday: 'They tried to kill us, we won, let's eat!'

★ ★ ★

Did you hear the one about the short-sighted circumciser?
He got the sack.

★ ★ ★

A blind man, a deaf man, and a paralysed man arrive in Heaven and are welcomed by Saint Peter.
'You blokes look like you need some help,' smiles Saint Peter. 'There is a holy healing spring just three kilometres or so down that winding path.'
Delirious, all three men rush down the path and eventually arrive at an oasis of sparkling water.
The blind man splashes water on his eyes. He stands up staring in amazement, 'My God, I

can see!'

The deaf man splashes water on his ears, stands up and exclaims, 'My God, I can hear!' The paralysed man rolls his wheelchair into the spring, then backs out shrieking, 'Holy shit! I've got new tyres!'

★ ★ ★

A clergyman was walking down the street when he came upon a group of about a dozen boys, all around twelve or thirteen years old. The group surrounded a forlorn, but rather cute, dog. Concerned that the boys were hurting the dog, he went over and asked, 'Children, what are you doing with that dog?' One of the boys replied, 'This dog is just an old neighbourhood stray. We all want him, but

The Pope Walked Into a Bar One Day...

only one of us can take him home. So we've decided that whichever one of us can tell the biggest lie will get to keep the dog.'

Of course, the reverend was taken aback. 'You boys shouldn't be having a contest telling lies!' he exclaimed. He then launched into a long sermon against lying, beginning with, 'Lying is a sin. You should never, ever lie,' and ending with, 'why, when I was your age, I never told a lie.'

There was dead silence for about a minute. Just as the reverend was beginning to think he'd gotten through to them, the smallest boy gave a deep sigh and said, 'All right, give him the bloody dog.'

★ ★ ★

What's the difference between a rottweiler and a Jewish mother?
Eventually the rottweiler lets go.

★ ★ ★

Two nuns are driving through a cemetery late one night. All of a sudden there is a tremendous crash as a big vampire drops down out of a tree and lands on the car. Sister Eunice, very frightened, says to Sister Mary, 'Sister Mary, save us! Show him your cross!'

With that, Sister Mary rolls down the car window, leans out, looks the vampire right in the eye and says, 'Get your ugly @#$% arse off my car, buster!'

★ ★ ★

A priest is walking down the street one day, when he notices a small boy trying to press a doorbell. However, the doorbell was just out of his reach. After watching the boy's efforts for some time, the priest moves closer to the boy's position. He steps smartly across the street, walks up behind the little fellow and, placing his hand kindly on the child's

The Pope Walked Into a Bar One Day...

shoulder, leans over and gives the doorbell a ring.

Crouching down to the child's level, the priest smiles benevolently and asks, 'And now what do you say, my little man?'

The boy turns to the Father and yells, 'Now, mister, we run!'

★ ★ ★

Three Points to Prove That...
Jesus was Mexican
1. His first name was Jesus.
2. He was bilingual.
3. The authorities were always harassing him.

But then there were equally good arguments that...

Jesus was black
1. He called everybody brother.
2. He liked Gospel.
3. He couldn't get a fair trial.

But then there were equally good arguments that...
Jesus was Jewish
1. He went into his father's business.
2. He lived at home until he was thirty-three.
3. He was sure his mother was a virgin, and his mother was sure he was God.

But then there were equally good arguments that...
Jesus was Italian
1. He talked with his hands.
2. He had wine with every meal.
3. He used olive oil.

But then there were equally good arguments that...

The Pope Walked Into a Bar One Day...

Jesus was Irish
1. He never got married.
2. He was always telling stories.
3. He loved green pastures.

But perhaps the most compelling evidence supports the idea that...

Jesus was a woman
1. He had to feed a crowd at a moment's notice when there was nothing in the fridge.
2. He kept trying to get the message across to a bunch of men who JUST DIDN'T GET IT.
3. Even when he was dead, he had to get up because there was more work for him to do.

★ ★ ★

A Jewish boy comes home from school and tells his mother that he's been given a part in the school play. 'Wonderful!' she replied. 'What part is it?'
The boy answered, 'I play the part of the Jewish husband.'
The mother scowled and said, 'Go back and tell the teacher you want a speaking part!'

★ ★ ★

How many Jewish mothers does it take to change a light bulb?
(Sigh) Don't bother, I'll sit in the dark. I don't want to be a nuisance to anybody.

★ ★ ★

Jewish telegram: 'Begin worrying! Details to follow.'

★ ★ ★

Once upon a time, God went missing for six days. Eventually, Michael the archangel found him, resting on the seventh day. He enquired of God, 'Where have you been, buddy?'
God sighed a deep sigh of satisfaction and proudly pointed downwards through the clouds. 'Look, Michael, look what I've made.'
Archangel Michael looked puzzled and said, 'What is it?'
'It's a planet,' replied God, 'And I've put life on it. I'm going to call it Earth and it's going to be a great place of balance.'
'Balance?' asked Michael, still confused.
God began to explain, pointing to different parts of Earth. 'For example, Western Europe will be a place of great opportunity and wealth, while Eastern Europe is going to be poor. The Middle East, well, that'll be a spot

The Pope Walked Into a Bar One Day...

full of trouble and strife. Over there I've placed a continent of white people and over there is a continent of black people.' God continued, pointing to different countries. 'And over there, I call this place America. North America will be rich and powerful and cold, while South America will be poor, and hot and friendly. And the little spot in the middle is Central America, which is a hot spot. Can you see the balance?'

'Yes,' said the archangel, impressed by God's work. He pointed to a small land mass and asked, 'Explain that one, my Lord.'

'Ah,' said God. 'That's New Zealand, the most glorious place on Earth. There are beautiful mountains, gorges, rainforests, rivers, streams and an exquisite coastline. The people are attractive, intelligent and humorous, and they're going to be found travelling the world. They'll be extremely sociable, hard-working and high-achieving, and they will be known as diplomats and carriers of peace. I'm also going to give them super-human, unbeatable rugby players who will be admired and feared by all who come across them'.

Michael gasped in wonder and admiration, but then exclaimed, 'You said there would be balance, my Lord!'

God replied wisely, 'Sure, Michael. Just wait until you see the ugly, whingeing, sheep-rooting, Aussie bastards I'm putting next to them.'

★ ★ ★

Sister Gabrielle entered the convent at a very tender age. The abbess warned Sister Gabrielle that she was entering a silent abbey, and that she must not speak until the abbess directed her to do so.
Five years passed before the abbess said to her, 'Sister Gabrielle, you can now speak. However, you can utter only two words.'
Sister Gabrielle retorted, 'Hard bed.'
'I'm sorry to hear that,' the abbess replied. 'We will get you a better bed.'
After ten years, the abbess said, 'You have been at this convent for another five years, Sister Gabrielle. It is time for you to say another two words.'
'Cold food,' said Sister Gabrielle.
The abbess assured Sister Gabrielle that the food would be better in the future.
On the fifteenth anniversary of her arrival, Sister Gabrielle was again allowed to speak two words.
'I quit,' said Sister Gabrielle.
'It's probably best,' smiled the abbess. 'After all, you've done nothing but bitch and moan since you got here.'

★ ★ ★

The Dumb, the Blonde, and the Irish

A professor was conducting a lecture about emotions for his psychiatry students.
'Just to establish some parameters,' said the professor, 'tell me, Adam, what is the opposite of joy?'
'Sadness,' replied the student.
'And what is the opposite of depression, Tarni?'
'Elation.'
'Okay, we're going well at this. What is the opposite of woe, Toby?'
'I believe that's giddy-up,' Toby replied.

★ ★ ★

A woman asked the pharmacist what would help get rid of her husband's dandruff. He

recommended Head and Shoulders.
The next day she returned and he asked how the treatment was going.
'Well, fine, I suppose,' she said, 'only how do you give shoulder?'

★ ★ ★

A farmer from outside of Hamilton was giving his blonde wife some last-minute instructions before he headed off into town for the day.
'Now, there'll be a guy dropping by this afternoon to artificially inseminate one of the cows. I've put a nail by the stall with the cow that I want him to impregnate.'
Satisfied that she understood the instructions, the farmer headed off to town.
The wife went about her chores all morning, then in the afternoon there was a knock on the door. She opened it to find the guy had arrived to do the artificial insemination. She took him out to the barn and showed him the stall with the nail beside it.
'This is the cow,' she said.
'What's the nail for?' asked the guy.
She replied, 'I guess that's where you're supposed to hang your pants.'

★ ★ ★

The Dumb, the Blonde, and the Irish

Jake, the local wannabe comedian, was in good form at the pub one Saturday night. 'The bus stops and these two Jews get off...' he began. Suddenly, a bloke gets off his stool and protests, 'Look, mate, I'm Jewish and I'm sick and tired of hearing about two Jews doing this and two Jews doing that. Pick on some other mob for a change.'

'Okay,' said Jake. 'Point taken.' So he starts again. 'The bus stops and these two Maoris get off and one said, "So there we were at my son's bar mitzvah...".

★ ★ ★

Two brunettes stumble wearily into their base camp on Mt. Cook after a failed attempt on the summit. One explains that their ten companions – all blondes – are dead. Fitfully, she recounts how the women had all found themselves clinging precariously to a rope hanging from a crumbling ledge.

'It was obvious the rope wasn't going to hold for long,' continued the second brunette, 'we were both on the bottom, so we decided to sacrifice ourselves to give the rest of them a chance.'

'True heroism!' exclaimed the camp director. 'But what happened?'

More Great Kiwi Jokes

'Well, replied the first brunette, 'we told them our plan to let go, and they all clapped.'

★ ★ ★

The Dumb, the Blonde, and the Irish

A man comes home from work one night, and his wife throws her arms around his neck and says happily, 'Darling, I have great news: I'm a month overdue. I think we're going to have a baby! The doctor gave me a test today, but until we find out for sure, let's not tell anybody.'

The next day, a guy from the electric company rings the doorbell because the young couple haven't paid their last bill.

'Are you Mrs Brodie? You're a month overdue, you know!'

'How do YOU know?' stammers the young woman, confused and horrified.

'Well, it's in our files!' says the man from the electric company.

'What are you saying? "It's in your files?".

'Absolutely.'

'Well, let me talk to my husband about this tonight.'

That night, she tells her husband about the visit, and he, mad as a bull, rushes to the electric company office the first thing the next morning.

'What's going on here? You have it on file that my wife is a month overdue? What business is that of yours?' the husband shouts.

'Just calm down,' says the clerk, 'it's nothing serious. All you have to do is pay us.'

'PAY you? And if I refuse?'

'Well, in that case, sir, we'd have no option but to cut you off.'
'And what would my wife do then?' the husband asks.
'I don't know. I guess she'd have to use a candle.'

★ ★ ★

After having thirteen children, Rosa and Luigi decided they didn't want any more children. They went to the doctor to get some advice about birth control. The doctor gave them a box of condoms, and said that if they used them during sex, they wouldn't have any more children. Rosa and Luigi thanked the doctor, then went home.

Two months later they were back in the doctor's office. 'Well,' said the doctor. 'I don't know how you managed it, but Rosa is pregnant again. I really don't understand how this happened – did you use the condoms like I told you?'

'Yessa, doctor,' said Rosa. 'We followed alla de instructions – except that since we no have de organ, I put it on de tambourine.'

★ ★ ★

Seamus was drowning his sorrows with a few pints of Guinness down at the pub. 'I cannot believe it,' he moaned to his mate Patrick, 'the

The Dumb, the Blonde, and the Irish

missus has yet another bun in the oven, and we've got ten kids already! I'll bloody hang myself if this happens again.'
What do you know, one year later, Seamus was back at the pub, drowning his sorrows at his wife's twelfth pregnancy.
'Seamus, my friend, you said that you'd hang yourself if this happened again,' reminded Patrick.
'And usually I'm a man of my word,' replied Seamus, 'but as I was tying the noose, it suddenly occurred to me: maybe I'm hanging the wrong man!'

★ ★ ★

Celebrant to a blonde: 'Do you take this man to be your lawful wedded husband, in good times or in bad?'
The blonde replied, 'In good times.'

★ ★ ★

Two hunters from Reparoa had been trying to shoot a stag, but never succeeded despite years of trying. Finally, they came up with a foolproof plan. They hired a doe costume and learnt the mating call. The plan involved hiding in the costume, luring a stag in towards them, then blowing a hole in him.

More Great Kiwi Jokes

Setting themselves up on the edge of a clearing, the two don their costume and start moaning like a horny beast. Before long, their call is answered and a stag comes crashing out of the bush and into the clearing.

'Okay, let's get the bastard!' says the guy in the front.

'Damn! The zip's stuck!' curses the man in the back, after pulling at it frantically. 'What the Hell are we going to do now?'

'Well, I'm going to start eating grass,' the guy in the front replies, 'but you'd better brace yourself.'

★ ★ ★

A couple of Irish hunters are out in the bush when one of them falls to the ground. He

The Dumb, the Blonde, and the Irish

doesn't seem to be breathing, and his eyes are rolled back in his head. The other guy whips out his mobile phone and calls an ambulance. He gasps to the operator, 'My friend is dead! What can I do?'
The operator, in a calm, soothing voice says, 'Just take it easy. I can help. First, let's first make sure he's really dead.'
There is a silence, then a shot is heard.
The hunter says, 'Okay, now what?'

★ ★ ★

The New Zealand Government funnelled a million dollars into forming a research project to investigate how humans manage to survive under extreme circumstances. They selected a Kiwi, a Frenchman and a Japanese to participate in a study to see how different ethnic backgrounds could increase or decrease one's ability to survive in the wild.
Each person was assigned specific tasks to perform – the Kiwi was put in charge of shelter, the Frenchman in charge of food, and the Japanese in charge of supplies. The three men were flown to an island in the Pacific, and left there for six months to fend for themselves.
When the researchers returned half a year

later, they were astonished to find a beautiful mansion on the beach. The Kiwi came to greet them and show them around. The researchers were very impressed with what the Kiwi had done: there were polished floorboards, a neatly thatched roof and a lovely creamy coconut-based paint on the walls. The Kiwi showed the researchers into the kitchen, where the Frenchman was preparing dinner using a whole larder full of gourmet ingredients. The Frenchman showed the researchers out into the huge garden, filled with lettuces, carrots, mangoes, coconuts and a huge assortment of tropical fruit and vegetables.

The researchers told the Kiwi and the Frenchman how impressed they were at the home the two had set up, but asked where the Japanese had gone.

'Well,' replied the Kiwi, 'the truth is that we haven't seen him since the day you left us all here.'

Rather concerned, the scientists jumped in their vehicle and drove around to the jungle, where they got out and started their search. Not long after they had left the car they heard a strange noise. As they went closer to investigate, the Japanese leaped from behind a tree, shouting 'Supplise!'

★ ★ ★

The Dumb, the Blonde, and the Irish

Three guys are in prison after committing terrible crimes. They have been sentenced to solitary confinement for two years, but each has been granted one request before the doors are closed.

The first guy asks for a year's supply of bourbon. The prison wardens give him his bourbon and lock the door.

The second guy says to the wardens that he wants a woman, so the obliging wardens give him a woman and lock the door.

The third guy asks for a year's supply of smokes. They give him what he asked for and lock the door.

Two years later the wardens open the doors and let each of the fellows out. The first guy crawls out, a happy drunk.

The second guy struts out with the woman on his arm and proudly announces, 'We've fallen in love and we're going to get married.'

The third guy comes running out of his cell and desperately asks, 'Does anybody have a match?'

★ ★ ★

What's the difference between a lawyer and a prostitute?
A prostitute will usually stop screwing you when you're dead.

★ ★ ★

More Great Kiwi Jokes

A rich yank was on holiday in New Zealand and he met up with a farmer, Bluey, in the pub. They were discussing farming and the yank asked Bluey how big his farm was. 'Three hundred acres,' was the reply. The yank went on about how he would get in his car and drive for two days and nights just to get across his farm back home in the States. Bluey's reply was, 'Yeah, I had a car like that.'

★ ★ ★

A blonde, wanting to earn some money, decided to hire herself out as a handyperson-type and started canvassing a wealthy neighbourhood.

The Dumb, the Blonde, and the Irish

She went to the front door of the first house and asked the owner if he had any jobs for her to do.

'Well, you can paint my porch. How much will you charge?' he said.

The blonde replied, 'How about fifty bucks?'

The man agreed and told her that the paint and other materials that she might need were in the garage.

The man's wife, inside the house, heard the conversation and said to her husband, 'Does she realize that the porch goes all the way around the house?' The man replied, 'She should, she was standing on it.'

A short time later, the blonde came to the door to collect her money.

'You're finished already?' he asked, amazed.

'Yes,' the blonde answered, 'And I had paint left over, so I gave it two coats.'

Impressed, the man reached in his pocket for her money.

'And by the way,' the blonde added, 'it's not a Porch, it's a Ferrari.'

★ ★ ★

When her beloved pair of pet rabbits died, the old woman thought it'd be nice to put them on her mantelpiece, so she took them to the taxidermist to have them stuffed.

'I can stuff these, no worries,' said the taxidermist. 'Do you want them mounted?'
'No,' she sighed, 'just holding hands.'

★ ★ ★

Paddy was at the Auckland airport waiting to pick up a friend when he needed to relieve himself. He went into the toilets and was surprised to find a small hole in the wall with a sign above it that read 'Your Wife Away From Home?'
Since there was no one around, Paddy unzipped his pants, stuck his penis into the hole and put fifty cents in the slot. At once, he experienced a terrible pain and promptly withdrew his willy – but not promptly enough. There, neatly sewed on it was a button.

★ ★ ★

Seamus, a newly arrived immigrant from Ireland, was always being laughed at by his colleagues. One guy in particular, Mac, was especially mean – every morning he'd greet Seamus with, 'Hey, Seamus, you seen Ben?'
'Ben who?'
'Ben' down and kiss my arse!'
Sick of falling for the same joke every day, Seamus spoke of his woes to another colleague, who said to him, 'Well, you know what you should do? Next time you see him,

The Dumb, the Blonde, and the Irish

ask him if she's seen Eileen. He'll ask, "Eileen who?" and you'll say, "I lean over and you kiss my arse!".'

Carefully remembering his lines, Seamus went to work and looked for Mac. When he found him, he said, 'Hey, Mac, you seen Eileen?'

'No,' answered Mac, 'She ran off with Ben.'

Seamus frowned. 'Ben who?'

★ ★ ★

A blonde walks into a travel agency and asks for the special Caribbean tour. The agent says, 'Certainly' and asks the blonde to fill out some forms in the office next door. Just as she goes into the room, somebody hits her over the head and knocks her out.

Later on that day, another blonde walks into the same agency and asks for the same Caribbean tour. Again the agent sends her next door to fill out the special forms whereupon she gets hit over the head and knocked out.

When the two blondes wake up, they find themselves floating in the ocean, out of sight of land and on a small boat. One of the blondes looks at the other and asks, 'I wonder if they'll fly us back?'

The other replies, 'I don't think so. They didn't last year.'

★ ★ ★

As old Frank shuffled into the house of ill-repute one night, the madam looked him up and down.
'Say old man, what do you expect to do in here?'
'I expect to get laid,' he answered.
'Oh yeah?' she scoffed. 'And how old are you?'
'Ninety-six.'
The madam shook her head and said, 'Ninety-six? Old man, you've *had* it.'
Frank scratched his head. 'Really? In that case, how much do I owe you?'

★ ★ ★

Having just fallen from the twentieth storey of a high-rise apartment building in Auckland, the blonde lay bruised, shocked and sore on the footpath. A crowd quickly gathered and moments later a policeman pushed his way through.
'What happened?' he asked the blonde.
'I don't know,' she replied, 'I just got here myself.'

★ ★ ★

Seamus came home early from work one day to hear strange groaning sounds from upstairs. Investigating, he finds his best mate Patrick in bed with his wife.

The Dumb, the Blonde, and the Irish

'What the Hell is going on in here!' Seamus roars at them both.
His wife turns to Patrick and rolls her eyes, 'See, I told you there was nothing to worry about,' she says, 'he really is thicker than pig shit!'

★ ★ ★

She Was So Blonde...
- At the bottom of an application where it says 'sign here' she wrote 'Sagittarius'.
- She took the ruler to bed to see how long she slept.
- She sent a fax with a stamp on it.
- She told me to meet her at the corner of 'WALK' and 'DON'T WALK'.
- She tried to put M&Ms in alphabetical order.
- She sold the car for petrol money.
- When she went to the airport and saw a sign that said, 'Airport left' she turned around and went home.
- When she heard that 90% of all crimes occur around the home, she moved.
- She thought if she spoke her mind, she'd be speechless.
- She thought that she could not use her AM radio in the evening.

★ ★ ★

'Doctor, I can't stop singing "The Green Grass of Home"!' exclaimed the worried patient.
'It seems to me like you've got a severe case of "Tom Jones" syndrome,' replied the doc.
'Is that common?' asked the patient.
'Well, it's not unusual...'

★ ★ ★

Walking down the street one night, the blonde saw a sign that read: 'Please press bell for night watchman.' She did so, and a short while later the watchman appeared. He proceeded to unlock gate after gate, and shut down the alarm system.
'Well, what do you want?' snarled the watchman.
'I just want to know why you can't ring it yourself.'

★ ★ ★

The Dumb, the Blonde, and the Irish

A tourist in a Cairo market had been absorbed in watching a man grooming his camel with such care and devotion. In fact, he had dallied so long that he thought he might miss the rest of the party.

'Excuse me,' he asked the camel man, 'can you tell me the time?'

The Arab knelt on one knee and gently lifted the camel's testicles. 'Three minutes to four,' he announced.

The tourist was amazed. He could hardly contain himself as he rushed off to the rest of the tourist party.

'Hold the bus a moment,' he said. 'you've got to come and see this fellow tell the time by holding a pair of camel's balls.'

His incredulous friends followed him through

the market until they came to the camel man.
'What's the time?' asked the tourist again.
The Arab knelt on his knee. Gently lifting the testicles, he announced, 'Five past four.'
Everyone was amazed as they checked their watches.
'I'll give you twenty dollars if you will teach me your secret,' said the tourist.
The Arab pocketed the money and beckoned the tourist to kneel down beside him. He took the camel's balls gently in his hand and lifted them a little.
'Do you see the clock on top of the railway station over there?' he said.

★ ★ ★

After leaving the racetrack, Dale bumped into his mate Bluey on the bus. 'Hey, how's it going?' asked Bluey.
'Going? Mate, do you want to hear one of the most amazing things that ever happened? What's today's date?'
'It's the seventh of July.'
'Rightoh. The seventh day of the seventh month. I got to the track at seven minutes past seven. My daughter is seven years old today, and we live at number seven on Seven Street.'
'Let me guess,' said Bluey, 'you put everything you had on the seventh horse in the seventh race.'

The Dumb, the Blonde, and the Irish

'Yup.'
'And he won?'
Dale sighed. 'No. He came in seventh.'

★ ★ ★

'Tell me,' said the judge, 'just why you parked there?'
Paddy rose and said respectfully, 'Because your Honour, it said: "Fine for Parking".'

★ ★ ★

Unable to move his bowels, the immigrant went to visit the doctor.
The doctor wrote the man a prescription for a laxative and told the immigrant to return to the clinic in a few days time for a check-up.
When the immigrant showed up at the clinic for his appointment, the doctor asked, 'Have you moved yet?'
As the immigrant answered in the negative, the doctor doubled the dosage and made another appointment for the immigrant.
On the appointed day the immigrant returned for his check-up, whereupon the doctor asked him again if he had moved. The answer was still negative, so once again the doctor doubled the dose.
A few days later, the immigrant returned to the

clinic, but this time he had a wide smile on his face.
'I take it you've moved?' asked the doctor.
The immigrant nodded. 'I had to. My flat was full of shit.'

★ ★ ★

A man was travelling the world, and one day happened upon a group of natives who invited him to become a member of their tribe.
'To do so,' explained the leader of the tribe, 'you've got to drink five litres of seal blood, wrestle a polar bear, and have sex with a woman from the tribe.'
Anxious to become a member of the tribe, the man agreed and set out to complete his tasks. Several hours went by, and the natives were wondering what had happened to him. Finally the man returned, covered in blood and with his clothes torn.
'Well,' he boasted, 'I did it! I finished two of my tasks. Now just tell me where to find that woman you want me to wrestle.'

★ ★ ★

The Dumb, the Blonde, and the Irish

A spaceship landed next to a petrol station and the captain sent his first officer out to interview some of the Earthlings. The first officer went up to a petrol pump and said, 'Take me to your leader.' But nothing happened. Back on the spaceship he told the captain that the Earthlings wouldn't talk, they just stood there with a silly look on their faces and their dicks stuck in their ears.

★ ★ ★

After three continuous weeks on the road, the trucker pulls into a local brothel and slams $500 on the counter.
'Young lady,' he says to the woman at the desk, 'I want a really tough overcooked steak, and the ugliest sheila you've got.'
'Listen,' says the madam, 'for $500 you can have an a la carte meal and the most beautiful girl in the place.'
'Look here, sweetheart,' the trucker growls, 'I'm not feeling horny, I'm feeling bloody homesick!'

★ ★ ★

An American tourist on a trip to Uluru suddenly yelled, 'Stop the bus!' and scrambled to the front to get off. On a track just off the main road he had spotted an Aborigine with his ear to the ground.

'He must be one of those famous trackers they have out here,' thought the Yank as he ran back to the Aborigine. 'Can you tell me about the last people to pass this way?' enquired the Yank.

'Yeah,' answered the Aborigine. He pointed to the wheel tracks and said, 'It was a Ford utility.'

The Yank thought about this for a second and then asked, 'Anything else?'

The Aborigine nodded. 'Yeah. There were ten people in it. Three in the front and seven in the back.'

The Yank was really impressed, 'Anything else?' he asked.

'Yeah. The three in the front were blokes, and there were four women and three kids in the back. The truck was red with yellow hubcaps.'

This amazed the Yank. 'You can tell all that just by putting your ear to the ground?'

'Not really,' said the Aborigine. 'I just fell off the bloody thing.'

★ ★ ★

The Dumb, the Blonde, and the Irish

Kevin and Bruce were in desperate need of jobs, so they bought a newspaper and looked through the employment section. They found an advertisement stating the following: 'Two butlers needed for Scottish country manor. References a must.' The job sounded ideal, but the one problem was that they didn't have references. Solution? Easy. Kevin wrote Bruce's reference and Bruce wrote Kevin's. They then took a bus to the manor and offered the lady of the manor their references. But she waved them aside, saying, 'We'll get onto that later. First, I'd like to check your knees. Formal wear here means wearing kilts so if you would be so kind as to drop the tweeds.' The lads thought it a little strange, but they did as requested.

'Not bad,' she said. 'Now you can show me your testimonials.'

When they picked themselves up from the gravel driveway, Kevin said, 'You know what, Bruce? With a little more education we would have got that job.'

★ ★ ★

A migrant went for a job and was told he would have to pass an IQ test. When he asked what an IQ was, the employer explained that anyone with an IQ of 100 would be admitted

to university, but a bloke with an IQ of 50 wouldn't be able to tie-up his shoe laces.
'Oh,' said the migrant. 'So that's why so many Aussies wear thongs.'

★ ★ ★

'Do you smoke after sex?' asked Rob.
'I don't know, I've never looked,' replied Trudy.

★ ★ ★

An Irish guy gets home early from work and hears strange noises coming from the bedroom. He rushes upstairs to find his wife naked on the bed, sweating and panting!
'What's up?' he asks.
'I'm having a heart attack,' she cries.
So the bloke rushes downstairs to grab the phone, but just as he's dialling, his young son comes up and says, 'Daddy! Daddy! Uncle Ted's hiding in your closet and he's got no clothes on!'
The guy slams the phone down and storms upstairs into the bedroom, past his screaming wife, and rips open the wardrobe door. Sure enough, there is his brother Ted, totally naked, cowering on the floor.
'You rotten bastard,' says the husband, 'my woman's having a heart attack and you're

The Dumb, the Blonde, and the Irish

running around naked scaring the bloody kids!'

★ ★ ★

Paddy the Irishman was very overweight so his doctor encouraged him to go on a diet. 'I want you to eat normally for two days, then skip a day, and repeat this procedure for three weeks. Come in for another appointment and I'll weigh you – by then you should have lost at least five kilograms.'
Three weeks later, Paddy returned to the clinic and shocked his doctor – he'd lost at least fifteen kilograms.
'That's amazing,' said the doctor. 'You lost that much just by following my instructions?'
Paddy nodded. 'I thought I was going to drop dead!'
'From hunger?'
'No,' replied Paddy. 'From skipping.'

★ ★ ★

Two men – a builder and his apprentice - drove up to a timberyard. The apprentice went up to the shop assistant and said, 'I'd like some four-by-fours.'
The shop assistant wrinkled his forehead and said, 'You mean two-by-fours, don't you?'

The apprentice shook his head. 'Nah, I'm sure my boss said we needed four-by-fours.'
'Is that him in the ute?' asked the assistant.
The apprentice nodded in reply.
'Well, would you go out and check with him exactly how long you want them?'
The novice went over to the car and when he returned to the shop assistant he said, 'We're building a house; we want them forever.'

★ ★ ★

Paddy the Irish fellow walked into a pharmacy and, blushing a little, he said, 'Look mate, I admit it, I'm a virgin, but I've asked this chick out for a date and she's hot for me. I think I might get to do the deed with her tonight. So can you tell me how much the condoms are?'
The pharmacist replied, 'They're $5.95, plus tax.'
'Ah,' said Paddy, 'I always wondered how you keep them on.'

★ ★ ★

An Irishman saw a priest walking down the street. Noticing his collar, he stopped him and said, 'Excuse me, but why are you wearing your shirt backwards?'
The priest laughed, 'Because, my son, I am a

The Dumb, the Blonde, and the Irish

Father.'
The Irishman scratched his head, 'But I am a father too, and I don't wear my shirt backwards!'
Again, the priest laughed. 'But I'm a father of millions.'
The Irishman replied, 'Well, then you should wear your underwear backwards.'

★ ★ ★

Two Irish hunters were out looking for pheasant when they came upon the local farmer's daughter, sitting naked on a fence, sunning herself.
The first hunter asked, 'Are you game?'
She snapped her gum and sassily replied, 'I sure am, honey!'
So the second hunter shot her.

★ ★ ★

Shopping Rules for Check-out Chicks
1. Please stack the merchandise so that removing one item from the shelf is likely to cause an avalanche in the aisle. This not only keeps my physiotherapist in work, it allows the other shoppers to laugh at me, giving entertainment to all.

2. Please mumble the amount due and ignore me/give me a disgusted look when I ask for clarification.
3. After asking you to put all the cold items in the same bags, please disregard this directive. You should not only put them randomly into different bags, but hide them under large items as well, just to add to the mystery of it all.
4. Since you are intelligent enough to know that bread and eggs should not go in the bottom of the bag, do not be offended if I request that you not do so, even when the last ten trips to the same supermarket have resulted in this particular arrangement of instant French toast.
5. Remember that I am only an intruder in your store, and you could run the place much more efficiently if I would just stay home. You would never have to restock the shelves, do any price checks, or put my groceries into bags. I should be made to feel as if I am demanding and unreasonable for any question or request that I have. After all, I deserve to be treated like an outcast for interrupting your chatting with the other check-out chicks.

★ ★ ★

The Dumb, the Blonde, and the Irish

Paddy and Irene, an Irish couple, wanted to start a family, and decided they wanted their first child to be black. Nine months later, Irene gave birth to a bouncing healthy white girl. Rather disappointed, Irene asked a black man on the street why their baby was white and not black. Realising she was a slice short of a loaf, the man whispered in Paddy's ear 'Is your penis at least a foot long?'
Rather shamefacedly, Paddy admitted it wasn't.
'Well, is it at least four inches wide?'
Once again, Paddy had to shake his head.
'Well, pal, that's your problem! You're letting in too much light!'

★ ★ ★

After muddling his way through most of the lengthy written instructions on how to use the ATM, the elderly customer eventually got stuck and walked over to a bank officer. 'Excuse me,' said the customer, 'but I was wondering if you could help me out.'
'Sure,' replied the teller, 'just go right through that door.'

★ ★ ★

More Great Kiwi Jokes

Jeff and Joe were sitting at a bar drinking a few beers, when an attractive woman came over and sat herself next to Joe. The woman licked her lips and looked seductively at him. Joe, blushing a little, said out of the corner of his mouth to Jeff, 'I think she likes me. What should I do?'

Chewing on a pretzel, Jeff whispered back, 'I reckon the direct approach is the best. Show her your nuts.'

Turning to the woman, Joe stuck his fingers up his nose, crossed his eyes and stuck out his tongue.

★ ★ ★

Heard about the Irish lottery?
If you win you get $10 a year over a million years.

★ ★ ★

The Dumb, the Blonde, and the Irish

Rangi and Hemi were pissed off when they got to Eden Park for the Rugby Test to find the ground sold out. It was so crowded inside that there were huge queues for the toilets, especially the men's. At half-time blokes were forced to head for the fence and find a knot-hole to pee through.

Rangi and Hemi were still outside lamenting their bad luck when they noticed the odd dick being poked through the fence.

'Here's a chance to make a bob or two!' shouted Rangi.

He grabbed the first dick and yelled, 'Throw five bucks over the fence or I'll cut your bloody cock off!'

A five dollar note immediately fluttered over the fence.

'We're onto something here,' said Rangi to Hemi. 'Now you go that way and I'll meet you when we've done the whole ground.'

Twenty minutes later they meet.

'I've got fifty bucks,' grinned Rangi, 'how about you?'

'Not so good,' sighed Hemi. 'I got only forty bucks, but I did get three dicks!'

★ ★ ★

More Great Kiwi Jokes

Mike walks into a pub one night and sees two sexy chicks sitting at the bar. He orders a beer, and strikes up a conversation with one of them. Things are looking good and after about an hour or so, he says to her, 'You know, I'm really attracted to you. I'd love to take you home and spend the night with you.'

The woman smiles and says, 'I'm very flattered, but it has to be cool with my sister. You see, we are extremely close.' With that she nods her head down to her hips and Mike follows her eyes to see that the two women are joined together – they are Siamese twins. The girl turns and whispers to her sister Mike's proposition, and the sister nods in agreement. The three of them then leave the pub and head for the girls' place.

When they get there, Mike is told to undress, and the girl he's been chatting up all night does the same. All three of them get into bed and Mike and the girl begin making love. The other twin, feeling a bit bored, reaches under the bed and pulls out a saxophone, which she then proceeds to play. Mike and her sister ignore her and continue to make passionate love.

The following morning, Mike gets dressed, kisses the girl on her cheek, and goes home. A couple of weeks later, the girls go back to the place where they met Mike and see him

The Dumb, the Blonde, and the Irish

sitting at the bar again.
'Oh, look!' said one of the twins. 'There's Mike. Do you reckon he'll remember us?'

★ ★ ★

A man is in a dreadful car accident where his injuries are so horrific that not only does he die, but he is disfigured to such a degree that the doctor can't positively determine his identity. He suspects, however, that it's a local guy named William. So the doc calls up two guys, Lonnie and Eric, who are William's best friends. He asks them to come into the morgue as soon as they can to help identify the body.
Lonnie and Eric go to the morgue the next day. The doctor lifts the sheet so that they can see the corpse. The two friends peer down to look at the body and carefully, to the doctor's surprise, turn the body over to examine his flipside.
Lonnie and Eric shake their head and say to the doctor, 'That's definitely not our friend William.'
The doctor says, 'But how can you be sure?'
Lonnie says, 'Easy. Our friend William has two arseholes.'
The doctor looks mystified and says incredulously, 'No way! How would you know

a thing like that, anyhow?'
Eric says, 'Well, whenever the three of us went into town, we always heard people say, "Here comes William with those two arseholes!".'

★ ★ ★

Waka picks up a job in the city at a construction site, but he's got nowhere to stay. He sees an ad in the paper: 'Room, full board and meals, $100 per week.'
He thinks this is a pretty good deal, so visits the house. When the sheila answers the door he says, 'I'm Waka and I'm here for the $100 room.'
'No problem,' replies the lady, 'you look like an alright sort of bloke, Waka. You'd might as well move right in now.' And so he does.
The next morning, the landlady makes him a huge breakfast and gives him a giant Vegemite sandwich to take to work. Later that day, Waka returns home and says, 'Thanks very much for lunch, ma'am, but unfortunately it wasn't enough.'
So the next morning she prepares him three Vegemite sandwiches and two peanut butter sandwiches. That afternoon, Waka comes home again and complains that he was still hungry after lunch.
On the third morning, the landlady packs him

The Dumb, the Blonde, and the Irish

eight Vegemite sandwiches, five peanut butter sandwiches, three chicken sandwiches and a thermos of pumpkin soup. On his return, Waka sighs, 'Lunch was lovely, ma'am, but it still wasn't enough.'

'You're extraordinary!' exclaims the landlady. So that night, she goes to the bakery and gets an eight-foot long roll and cuts it down the middle. Into it she stuffs a whole chicken, half a leg of lamb, three beef rissoles, seven onions, eight potatoes, six heads of lettuce, a dozen eggs, a turnip, nine bacon rinds and two beetroot. In the morning, she wraps it up and sends Waka on his way with his enormous submarine.

He arrives home from work that afternoon and the landlady asks him, 'So how was lunch today?'

'Lovely,' replies Waka. 'However, I notice that you are back to just one sandwich again.'

★ ★ ★

More Great Kiwi Jokes

What happened when Mick from Ireland was told he'd been promoted from standard three to standard four in primary school?
He was so excited he cut himself shaving.

★ ★ ★

'Okay, Madeleine,' the teacher said to her standard two pupil. 'Let's see you count.'
Holding out her hand, Madeleine counted off her fingers, 'One, two, three, four, five.'
Smiling, the teacher said, 'Well done, Madeleine, but can you count any higher?'
Lifting her hand over her head, Madeleine started over again.

★ ★ ★

It had been some time since the overweight woman had had a date, so she went to a psychiatrist.
'Why don't you diet?' suggested the psychiatrist upon hearing the woman's dating woes.
The young woman thought for a minute and then said, 'Now that's a thought. What colour?'

★ ★ ★

The Dumb, the Blonde, and the Irish

Ben the builder was rushed to the hospital one day, his foot wrapped in bandages and bleeding profusely.

'What happened?' asked the doctor.

'Well,' began Ben, 'fifteen years ago, I began as a builder's apprentice in Palmerston North, and I...'

'Wait man, fifteen years ago? What about your foot?'

'I'm getting to that, just hold on,' snapped Ben. 'Anyway, I was learning my trade under a builder named Harry, and I was living in his house. The night that I moved into his house, his gorgeous daughter Tamara came in to my room wearing a skimpy, sexy nightgown, and said to me, "Is there anything I can do for you, Ben?" And I said, "No, thank you, Tamara, I have everything I need; I am fine." The next night she came back wearing that sexy little piece again, and was wearing this lovely perfume that made her smell like a blossoming rose. And she said, "Ben, is there anything at all I can do for you?"

And I said, "No, thank you kindly, Tamara, I have everything I need; I am fine."

The next night she came in starkers and asked me again, "Is there anything at all I can do for you, sweetest Ben?" And I said to her, "Thanks very much, Tamara, but I have everything I need; I'm fine.".'

More Great Kiwi Jokes

The doctor shifted impatiently and sighed in exasperation. 'But what does this have to do with your foot?'
Ben rolled his eyes and scowled. 'Well, this morning, I finally figured out what she meant, and I got so angry at my stupid self that I threw down a hammer and busted my foot!'

★ ★ ★

After having a terrible game, the AFL team returned to the field after half-time. Going into a huddle, they suddenly dropped their pants and began jerking off. Horrified, the coach called one of the full-forwards over, 'What the HELL are you guys doing out there?' he shrieked.
The full-forward replied, 'Coach, we're just doing what you told us.'
The coach was baffled, 'What do you mean?'
'Back in the locker room, you told us to go back out and pull ourselves together.'

★ ★ ★

A Kiwi couple, a French couple and an Australian couple were out dining one Saturday night. The Kiwi bloke said to his date, 'Would you pass me the sugar, sweetie?' Smiling lovingly at his own companion, the

The Dumb, the Blonde, and the Irish

Frenchman said to his date, 'Would you pass me the salt, honey?'
Wanting to look as romantic as the other men, the Aussie said to his date, 'Would you pass me the cream, cow?'

★ ★ ★

Having married shortly before Easter, the couple were honeymooning in a cottage over the Easter holidays. In bed, the man began to cuddle his wife, but she didn't respond.
'I'm sorry, love,' she said, 'but I can't make love to you now.'
'Why?' he demanded crossly.
'Because it's Lent,' she replied.
Furious, the husband screamed, 'Oh yeah? To who and for how long?'

★ ★ ★

Walking down the street, the Irishman noticed a sign in a shoe repair shop: BOOTS POLISHED INSIDE. Going in, he went up to the shop assistant and said, 'I don't need my boots polished, but I've got a question. How do you keep the polish from getting on people's socks?'

★ ★ ★

Filling out a job application, the Irishman was flummoxed when he came to the question 'sex'. After ticking the 'M' and 'F' boxes, he wrote in the margin, 'And sometimes we shag on Wednesday, too.'

★ ★ ★

At the publishing party, the novelist began talking to the famous literary critic.
'So tell me, what did you think of my new book?' he asked the critic. 'Your opinions carry a lot of weight, you know.'
The critic sniffed. 'The truth is, it's without merit.'
The novelist replied, 'Oh, I know. But I'd love to hear it just the same.'

★ ★ ★

Walking into a pharmacy, a little inner-city boy asked the shop assistant for a packet of tampons. The woman smiled, 'Are these for your sister?'
'No,' the boy replied. 'For me.'
'Whatever for?' asked the assistant, perplexed.
'It said on television that if you used tampons, you could swim, skate, go climbing and do lots of other cool things.'

★ ★ ★

The Dumb, the Blonde, and the Irish

Mick the Irish bloke goes into a pub and orders himself a beer. He spots two women drinking at a table nearby and orders them a round of drinks, too.
'Hey, Mick, don't waste your money,' said the bartender. 'Those two are lesbians.' Mick replies, 'Hey, no worries, buy them a drink and put it on my tab.'
After he finishes his beer he says to the bartender, 'Another beer for me and another round for the girls.'
'You're wasting your money, Mick, I'm telling you, those chicks are lesbians.'
'Aw, don't try to spoil my fun, get them another drink and add it to my tab.'
This continues for three more rounds and finally, with beer-induced confidence, Mick brushes his hand through his hair, clears his throat and walks over to the ladies. He suavely pulls up a chair, smiles and says, 'So, ladies, which part of Lesbia are you from?'

★ ★ ★

Irish Air Flight 201 was flying from Glasgow to Dublin one night, with Paddy, the pilot, and Sean the co-pilot. As they approached Dublin airport, they looked out the front window.
'Bejeesus' said Paddy. 'Will ye look at how short that runway is!'
'You're not kiddin', Paddy,' replied Sean.
'This is gonna be one of the trickiest landings you're ever gonna see,' said Paddy. 'You're not kiddin', Paddy,' replied Sean.
'Right, Sean. When I give the signal, you put the engines in reverse,' directed Paddy.
'Right, then, I'll be doing that,' replied Sean.
'And then you put the flaps down straight away,' said Paddy.
'Right, then, I'll be doing that,' replied Sean.
'And then you stamp on those brakes as hard as ye can,' said Paddy.
'Right, then, I'll be doing that,' replied Sean.
'And then ye pray to God with all of your soul,' said Paddy.
'I be doing that already,' replied Sean.
So they approached the runway with Paddy and Sean's brows trickling with nervous sweat. As soon as the wheels hit the ground, Sean put the engines in reverse, dropped the flaps down, stamped on the brakes and prayed to God with all of his soul. Amidst roaring engines, squealing of tyres and lots of smoke, the plane screeched to a halt just centimetres

The Dumb, the Blonde, and the Irish

from the end of the runway, much to the relief of Paddy and Sean and everyone on board. As they sat in the cockpit regaining their composure, Paddy looked out the front window and said to Sean, 'That has gotta be the shortest runway I have ever seen in my whole life.'
Sean looked out the side window and replied: 'Yeah, Paddy, but look how wide it is.'

★ ★ ★

One day there was a huge explosion in an ammunitions factory, and once all the mess had been cleared up the police began an inquiry into the accident. A policeman was appointed to spend all morning interviewing the workers at the factory and one of them was Harry.
'Okay, Harry,' said the policeman, 'you are a witness, what happened?'
'Well, it's like this,' replied Harry. 'Old Robbie was in the gunpowder room, and I saw him take a cigarette out of his pocket and light up.'
'He was smoking in the gunpowder room?' the investigator said incredulously. 'How long had he been with the company?'
'About twenty years, sir,' said Harry.
'Twenty years in the company, then he goes and strikes a match in the gunpowder room?

I'd have thought it would be the *last* thing he'd have done.'
'It was, sir.'

★ ★ ★

A traffic policeman pulled alongside a speeding car on the motorway.
Glancing at the car, he was astounded to see that the blonde behind the wheel was knitting. After following her for several miles with the lights flashing and the siren wailing, he started yelling at the woman over a megaphone, 'Pull over, ma'am! I say pull over!'

Eventually the blonde pulled to the side of the road.

The Dumb, the Blonde, and the Irish

Rushing up to her car, the policemen yelled through the window, 'Oi! Didn't you hear me say "pull over!"?'
'Yeah, but you were wrong!' the blonde yelled back. 'It's not a pull over, it's a scarf!'

★ ★ ★

Naughty Stuff

One day a mother was cleaning her teenage son's room and in the closet she found a bondage sadomasochist magazine. This was highly upsetting for her, so she took the magazine away and showed it to her husband when he got home from work.
Her husband looked at the magazine, grimaced, and handed it back to her without a word. So she asked him, 'What should we do about this?'
Her husband sighed and said, 'Well, I don't think you should spank him.'

★ ★ ★

Naughty Stuff

Two old ladies, Gertie and Agatha, were outside their nursing home having a smoke when it started to rain. Gertie pulled out a condom, cut off the end, put it over her cigarette, and continued smoking. Agatha was perplexed.
'What's that?' she asked, peering closer for a better look.
Gertie replied, 'Oh, just a condom. This way my cigarette doesn't get wet.'
Agatha asked her where she got them.
'Oh, just go to a chemist; no worries,' replied Gertie.
The next day, Agatha went into a chemist and asked the pharmacist for a box of condoms. He looked at her kind of strangely (she was, after all, over 80 years of age), but politely asked what brand she preferred.
She replied, 'It doesn't matter, dear, just so long as it fits a Camel.'

★ ★ ★

Dan said to his wife the other day, 'Hey honey, let's go out and have some fun.'
She replied, 'Okay, but if you get home before I do, leave the back door open.'

★ ★ ★

More Great Kiwi Jokes

The well-presented salesman was doing his rounds up and down the streets of Christchurch when he bumped into a businessman carrying a briefcase.
He said, 'Sir, would you like to buy a toothbrush for ten dollars?'
Shocked, the man said, 'You kidding? I doubt it, man. That's highway robbery!'
The salesman was hurt. 'Well, then, how about a homemade brownie for ten cents?'
This was a better deal, so the man handed ten cents to the salesman and received the brownie in exchange. Unwrapping the brownie, he took a bite and immediately spat out a mouthful.
'This tastes like shit!' he sputtered.
'It is,' said the salesman, 'so, do you want to buy a ten dollar toothbrush?'

★ ★ ★

A husband and wife are in bed watching 'Who Wants to be a Millionaire?'
'Hey, honey,' says the husband. 'Let's get down under the blankets. You up for it?'
The wife says, 'No.'
Her husband asks, 'Is that your final answer?'
She responds, 'Yes.'
He says, 'Then, I'd like to call a friend.'

★ ★ ★

Naughty Stuff

One Saturday morning, a woman went to a pet shop and immediately spotted a beautiful parrot in a cage near the door. There was a sign on the cage that said $20. 'Why so cheap?' she asked the pet shop owner.

The owner replied, 'Look, I should tell you first that this bird used to live in a brothel, and sometimes it says some pretty vulgar stuff. That's why I've had to mark her price down.'

The woman thought about this, but decided she had to have the bird anyway. She took it home and hung the cage up in her living room and waited for the bird to say something.

The bird looked around the room, then at her, and said, 'New house, new madam.' The woman was a bit shocked at the implication, but then thought, 'Oh well, I guess that doesn't really matter.'

When her two teenage daughters returned from school the bird saw them and said, 'New house, new madam, new whores.'

The girls thought it was a scream. The mother was offended once more, but brushed it off and began laughing with her daughters.

Moments later, the woman's husband came home from work. The bird looked at him and said, 'Hi, Eric.'

★ ★ ★

More Great Kiwi Jokes

Upon being asked to explain the secret behind his successful forty-year marriage, Eliot replied, 'The true secret of a long-lasting marriage is commitment. We are both very committed to making our marriage work, to being happy together. I can tell you though, it doesn't just happen instantly without effort. We make time for love. For instance, one night a week we go to a nice little restaurant for a romantic candlelight dinner. There's some red wine to be had and following on from that, of course, is some cheek-to-cheek dancing, followed by a long night of very intense and passionate lovemaking. She goes Tuesdays, I go Thursdays.'

★ ★ ★

Old Cliffy was the oldest man ever to compete in the Olympic Games, and was a hot interview subject with the reporters. When asked about his athletic prowess Old Cliffy replied, 'It's in my genes. Me dad's over a hundred years old and he still does laps at the local oval. The only reason he's not here rooting for me is because he's the best man at my grandad's wedding.'
'How old is your grandfather?' asked the reporter, incredulous.

Naughty Stuff

'He's just turned 132.'
'Wow,' gasped the reporter. 'I can't imagine wanting to get married at that age.'
'Want's got nothing to do with it,' said Old Cliffy with a wink, 'see, Grandad *has* to get married.'

★ ★ ★

A young bloke was enjoying his first night in a Munich beer house when a pretty young lady sat beside him.
'Hello,' he said. 'Do you understand English?'
'Only a little,' she answered.
'How much?' he asked.
'Fifty dollars,' she replied.

★ ★ ★

What do bungee jumping and hookers have in common?
They both cost a hundred bucks and if the rubber breaks, you're screwed.

★ ★ ★

A little boy walks into his parents' room to see his mum on top of his dad bouncing up and down. He quickly runs out of the room. The mum spots her son and quickly dismounts,

worried about what he might have seen. She dresses quickly and goes to find him.
The son asks, 'What were you and Dad doing?'
The mother replies, 'Well, you know Daddy has a big tummy and sometimes I have to get on top of it to help flatten it.'
'You're wasting your time,' says the boy.
'Why is that?' asks his mum, puzzled.
'Well, when you go shopping, the lady next door comes over and gets on her knees and blows it right back up.'

★ ★ ★

What doesn't belong on this list: meat, eggs, wife, blow job?
Blow job: You can beat your meat, eggs or wife, but you can't beat a blow job

★ ★ ★

Tali-Amber had a problem and eventually decided to see a psychiatrist about it.
'You have to do something to help me!' she wailed to Dr Feelgood. 'Every time I go on a date, I always end up doing all kinds of weird, perverted sexual acts. And then I spend the next day feeling guilty as Hell about it.'
'I understand, dear,' said Dr Feelgood. 'We'll

Naughty Stuff

have a few sessions together so that we can work on your willpower.'
'No!' she responded vehemently. 'I want you to work on getting rid of the guilt.'

★ ★ ★

Carey thought he'd give his wife something really special on her thirty-fifth birthday. When the day rolled around, he gave her this really nice, romantic card in which he had written that she could have two hours of the wildest sex she'd ever had in her life. No restrictions, absolutely anything goes.
On her birthday, Carey's wife smiled, gave him a hug and bolted out the front door, yelling over her shoulder as she went, 'I'll see you in two hours.'

★ ★ ★

What's the difference between a cheap hooker and an elephant?
One lies on its back for peanuts. The other lives at the zoo.

★ ★ ★

What's the difference between a sewing machine and a lady jogging?'
The sewing machine has just one bobbin.

★ ★ ★

A psychic convention was held in the Auckland Town Hall one night. The MC says to the audience, 'Ladies and gentlemen, so that we can realise the common bond we have with each other, I ask for a show of

Naughty Stuff

hands – would anyone who has ever heard a voice from the other side please raise their hands.'
At that, two hundred hands go up.
'Now, would anybody who has seen a spirit from the other side please raise their hands.'
At this about one hundred hands go up.
'Would anyone who has ever spoken with, or had any kind of two-way communication with a spirit from the other side – for instance, a ghost, please raise their hands.'
This time only ten hands are raised.
The MC then asked, 'Now, tell me, have any of you ever had any kind of sexual experience with a ghost?'
After a long minute of silence, a small hand timidly rises at the very back of the room. The hand belongs to a farm boy named Marvin.
'You, sir, would you please come up on the stage?' said the MC.
Very shyly, Marvin slowly walked from the back of the room up onto the stage.
The MC then said, 'Sir, this is amazing. You mean to tell us that you have actually had sexual intercourse with a ghost?'
Marvin smiled apologetically and said, 'I'm sorry – I thought you said goat!'

★ ★ ★

More Great Kiwi Jokes

What do you call an Aussie with twenty girlfriends?
A shepherd.

★ ★ ★

Heard about the new use they found for sheep in Australia?
Wool.

★ ★ ★

Naughty Stuff

Young King Arthur was ambushed and imprisoned by the monarch of a neighbouring kingdom. The monarch could have killed him, but was moved by Arthur's youth and ideals. So the monarch offered him freedom, as long as he could answer a very difficult question. Arthur would have a year to figure out the answer; if, after a year, he still had no answer, he would be put to death. The question: What do women really want?

Such a question would perplex even the most knowledgeable man, and, to young Arthur, it seemed an impossible query. But, since it was better than death, he accepted the monarch's proposition to have an answer by year's end. He returned to his kingdom and began to poll everybody: the princesses, the prostitutes, the cooks, the priests, the wise men, the serving wenches, the court jester. He spoke with everyone, but no one could give him a satisfactory answer. Many people advised him to consult the old witch - only she would know the answer. The price would be high; the witch was famous throughout the kingdom for the exorbitant prices she charged.

The last day of the year arrived, and Arthur had no alternative but to talk to the witch. She agreed to answer his question, but he'd have to accept her price first: The old witch wanted to marry Sir Gawain, the most noble of the

Knights of the Round Table and Arthur's closest friend! Young Arthur was horrified: she was hunchbacked and hideous, had only one tooth, smelled like sewage, made obscene noises, etc. He had never encountered such a repugnant creature. He refused to force his friend to marry her, and have to endure such a burden.

Sir Gawain, upon learning of the proposal, spoke with Arthur. He told him that nothing was too big a sacrifice compared to Arthur's life and the preservation of the Round Table. Hence, their wedding was proclaimed, and the witch answered Arthur's question thus: what a woman really wants is to be in charge of her own life. Everyone instantly knew that the witch had uttered a great truth and that Arthur's life would be spared. And so it was. The neighbouring monarch granted Arthur total freedom.

What a wedding Sir Gawain and the witch had! Arthur was torn between relief and anguish. Gawain was proper as always, gentle and courteous. The old witch put her worst manners on display, and generally made everyone very uncomfortable.

The honeymoon hour approached. Sir Gawain, steeling himself for a horrific experience, entered the bedroom. But what a sight awaited him! The most beautiful woman

Naughty Stuff

he'd ever seen lay before him! The astounded Sir Gawain asked what had happened. The beauty replied that since he had been so kind to her when she'd appeared as a witch, she would henceforth be her horrible, deformed self half the time, and the other half, she would be her beautiful maiden self. Which would he want her to be during the day, and which during the night?

What a cruel question! Sir Gawain pondered his predicament. During the day, he could have a beautiful woman to show off to his friends, but at night, in the privacy of his home, he'd share his bed with an old witch? Or would he prefer having by day a hideous witch, but by night a beautiful woman with whom to enjoy many intimate moments? The noble Sir Gawain replied that he would let her choose for herself.

Upon hearing this, she announced that she would be beautiful all the time, because he had respected her enough to let her be in charge of her own life.

What is the moral of this story?

If your woman doesn't get her own way, things are going to get ugly!

★ ★ ★

Mark goes to see a psychiatrist. The shrink, in an attempt to analyse him, pulls out some paper and says to Mark, 'I'm going to show you some inkblots and I want you to tell me the very first thing that pops into your mind when you see each one.'

He shows Mark the first drawing and Mark says, 'Ooooh, hot, dirty sex.' And gives the same reply for the next inkblot, and the one after that.

The psychiatrist says, 'Well, you certainly seem to be a little obsessed with sex.' Mark says indignantly, 'Me? You're the pervert with all the dirty pictures!'

★ ★ ★

There were two gay guys living together in a flat in Wellington. One of them had absolutely no chest hair and it really bothered him. So, one day he decided to ask his naturopath what was wrong with him. The naturopath said the only thing he could do to stimulate hair growth was to smother Vaseline all over his chest daily. The guy was overjoyed — finally, he would have chest hair! He went home and immediately slathered his chest with Vaseline.

When his boyfriend came home and jumped

Naughty Stuff

into bed with him, he felt the Vaseline and asked, 'What's this crap all over your chest?'
'The doctor said if I put Vaseline on my chest I'd be able to grow some hair there.'
'You idiot,' laughed his boyfriend. 'Just think about it, man. If that were true you'd have a ponytail coming out of your arse by now.'

★ ★ ★

Three old blokes were sitting on a park bench when a pretty jogger went past. The first old chap said, 'If I was younger, I'd jump up and give her a big cuddle.'
The second old bloke said, 'If I was younger, I'd jump up and give her a big cuddle and then a passionate kiss.'
The third old chap said, 'If I was younger I'd jump up and give her a big cuddle and then a passionate kiss, throw her on the ground, rip her shorts off and... what was that other thing we used to do?'

★ ★ ★

A woman went into a sex shop and asked for a vibrator.
'Certainly, madam,' said the assistant, beckoning the woman with a motion of her index finger. 'Come this way.'
'If I could come that way,' said the woman, 'I wouldn't need a vibrator.'

★ ★ ★

The trucker couldn't believe it. There, in the middle of the desert was a flashing neon sign: 'Mama's Desert Diner'. He had crossed this desolate stretch many times and never seen it before. He went in and spoke to the woman at the counter.

Naughty Stuff

'Yes, we're new here,' informed Mama. 'What will you have?'
'Two hamburgers and a hot dog,' he ordered.
He saw Mama go to the fridge, reach for two rissoles and whack them up under her armpits.
Horrified, the trucker cried, 'What are you doing that for?'
'Everything is deep frozen out here,' she explained. 'That's the only way I can thaw them out.'
'Well, okay,' said the reluctant trucker, 'but cancel the hot dog.'

★ ★ ★

A captain in the foreign legion was transferred to a desert outpost in central Australia. On his tour of the area he noticed a very old, sickly camel tied up in the back of the enlisted men's barracks. He asked the sergeant leading the tour what the camel was for.
The sergeant replied, 'Well, sir, it's a long way from anywhere, and the men have natural sexual urges, so when they do, uh, we have the camel.'
The captain chirped, 'Well, if it's good for morale, then I guess it's all right with me!'
After he had been at the fort for about six months the captain couldn't stand his starved-

for-sex life any longer and said to the
sergeant, 'Um, would you mind bringing me
the camel?'

The sergeant shrugged his shoulders and led
the camel into the captain's quarters. The
captain then proceeded to have himself a bit,
and said, 'Those guys are onto a good thing
with this camel!'

The sergeant replied, 'Well, sir, you're right
there. But they usually just use the camel to
ride into town.'

★ ★ ★

A small boy asks his dad, 'I heard a new word
on the TV: politics. What's that word mean,
Dad?'

His dad replies, 'Well son, that's a good
question. Let me try to explain it. I'm the
breadwinner of the family, so let's call me
"capitalism". Your mum, she's the
administrator of the money, so we'll call her
"the government". We're here to take care of
your needs, so we'll call you "the people". The
babysitter, let's see now, yes, we'll call her
"the working class". And your baby sister
Janie, we'll call her "the future". Now think
about that and see if it makes sense.'

So the little boy goes off to bed thinking about
what his father has said.

Naughty Stuff

Later that night, he hears his baby sister crying, so he gets up to check on her. He finds that the baby has severely soiled her nappy. So the little boy goes to his parents' room and finds his mother sound asleep. Not wanting to wake her, he goes to the babysitter's room. Finding the door locked, he peeks in the keyhole and sees his father in bed with the babysitter. He gives up and goes back to bed.

The next morning, the little boy says to his father, 'Dad, I think I understand the concept of politics now.'

The father says, 'Good, son, tell me in your own words what you think politics is all about.'

The little boy replies, 'Well, while capitalism is screwing the working class, the government is sound asleep, the people are being ignored and the future is in deep shit.'

★ ★ ★

The standard three teacher said, 'Today, children, we're going to play a game. I'm going to hold something behind my back and describe it to you, and you have to guess what it is.'

Reaching into her desk, she picked up an object and held it behind her. 'This is round

and yellow,' she said.
'A tennis ball?' asked Janie.
'No,' said the teacher, 'it's a lemon. But it shows you were thinking.'
She reached into her desk again and withdrew another object. 'Now who can guess what this is? It's long and yellow.'
'A banana?' asked Cassie.
'No,' said the teacher. 'It's a pencil. But it shows you were thinking.'
Matthew then raised his hand from the back of the classroom. 'Hey, Miss, can I try doing one?' The teacher said that would be fine, and Matthew turned his back on the class. 'Okay,' he said, 'listen everybody, what I've got in my hand is an inch long and has a red tip.'
'Matthew!' said the teacher, shocked.
'It's just a match,' said Matthew. 'But it shows you were thinking!'

★ ★ ★

How many Aussies does it take to change a light bulb?
One, but you have to pry him off the sheep first.

★ ★ ★

Naughty Stuff

Mrs Somers was at the funeral home where her husband's corpse was being prepared for viewing. She said to the embalmer, 'You're doing a great job there. He looks very handsome, but I'm afraid you've made a bit of a mistake.'
'How so?' asked the embalmer.
'Well, I'm afraid that you've put my husband's grey suit on the man over there in the corner, and my husband is wearing someone else's suit.'
The embalmer was mortified. 'Oh, I'm terribly sorry. What a terrible mistake! I do beg your forgiveness. If you'll just step outside for a moment I will correct my mistake.'
About five minutes later, he invited Mrs Somers back into the room to see that her husband now had the correct suit on.
'That's amazing,' said Mrs Somers. 'How did you manage to do it so fast?'
'Simple,' the embalmer replied. 'I just switched heads.'

★ ★ ★

There was this kid, about fifteen years old, walking down the street dragging a flattened frog on a string behind him. He came up to a house of ill repute and rapped on the door. When the madam answered it, she at once

More Great Kiwi Jokes

saw the flattened frog and thought the boy was a little odd. But she was used to odd people, so she asked the boy what he wanted. The kid snapped, 'I want to have sex with one of the women inside. I have plenty of money to pay for it, and I'm not going to leave until I get it.'

The madam figured why not, so she let the boy inside and said he could choose any of the girls he liked.

The boy asked, 'Do any of the girls have any diseases?' Of course the madam said no. He said, 'I heard all the men talking about having to get VD treatment after making love with Tiffany. She's the girl I want.'

He was so adamant on the issue that the madam just shrugged and agreed. She told him to go down the hall. He went into the room, still trailing the flattened frog behind him.

Ten minutes later he came back, still dragging the frog, paid the madam, and headed out the door. The madam stopped him and asked, 'Why did you pick the only girl in this place with VD, when you could've had any girl here?'

The boy answered, 'Well, if you must know, tonight when I get home, my parents are going out to a restaurant to eat, leaving me at home with a babysitter. After they leave, my

Naughty Stuff

babysitter will have sex with me because she just happens to be very fond of cute teenage boys. She will then get the disease that I just caught. When Mum and Dad get back, Dad will take the babysitter home. On the way, he'll jump the babysitter's bones, and he'll catch the disease. Then when Dad gets home from the babysitter's, he and Mum will go to bed and have sex, and Mum will catch it. In the morning when Dad goes to work, the milkman will deliver the milk, have a quickie with Mum and catch the disease, and he's the son-of-a-bitch who ran over my @#$% frog!'

★ ★ ★

On Wednesday night, Cameron, who had been married for six years, was having dinner with a young woman he'd been having an affair with. He said to her, 'Answer me this, love. What would you do if you suddenly found yourself pregnant with my child, and abandoned?'
'Why,' she said, 'I think I'd darn well kill myself!'
Sitting back contentedly, the man sighed and said, 'Good girl.'

★ ★ ★

More Great Kiwi Jokes

A Russian is strolling along a Moscow street and kicks a bottle in the gutter. Before the Russian can do anything, a genie suddenly wafts out from the bottle. The Russian is stunned as the genie says, 'Hello, master, I will grant you one wish, for I am here to serve you.'

The Russian thinks for a moment and then says, 'I wish to drink vodka whenever I want, so make me piss vodka.' And the genie grants him his wish.

When the Russian gets home he gets a glass out of the cupboard and pisses into it. He looks at the glass and it's clear. Looks like vodka. Then he smells the liquid. Smells like vodka. So he takes a taste and it is the best vodka that he has ever tasted. The Russian yells to his wife, 'Natasha, Natasha, come quickly.'

She comes running down the hall and the Russian takes another glass out of the cupboard and pisses into it. He tells her to drink, that it is vodka. Natasha is reluctant, but goes ahead and takes a sip. It is the best vodka that she has ever tasted. The two drink and party all night.

The next night the Russian comes home from work and tells his wife to get two glasses out of the cupboard. He proceeds to piss in the two glasses. The result is the same, the vodka

Naughty Stuff

is excellent and the couple drink until the sun comes up.
Finally, Friday night comes, and the Russian tells his wife to grab one glass from the cupboard. She gets the glass but asks him, 'Boris, why do we only need one glass?' Boris raises the glass and says, 'Because tonight, my love, you drink from the bottle.'

★ ★ ★

How can you tell if your wife is dead?
The sex is the same, but the dishes start piling up.

★ ★ ★

A girl from the poorer side of town goes to Social Security to register for childcare benefits. 'How many kids have you got?' asked the human development officer.
'Twelve,' replied the girl.
'Twelve?' replied the officer incredulously. 'What are their names?'
'Billy, Billy, Billy, Billy, Billy, Billy, Billy, Billy, Billy, Billy, Billy and Billy.'
'But doesn't that get confusing?'
'Nah,' said the girl. 'It's great because if they

are out playing in the street, I just have to shout, "Billy, your dinner's ready!" or "Billy, do your homework!" and they all do it.'
'What if you want to speak to one individually?' asked the officer.
'Easy,' said the girl. 'I just use their surnames.'

★ ★ ★

A man was prescribed Viagra for a little problem that he was experiencing. The prescription advice was to take it one hour before having sex. So he hurried home and waited for his wife to arrive from work. An hour before she was due home, he took the pills. But just as he was expecting his wife to walk through the door, she rang him to say that she'd be held up at work for another two hours.
Panicking, he telephoned the pharmacist.
'What should I do?' he asked. 'I've taken Viagra and am feeling incredibly toey, but the effects will have worn off before my wife arrives home!'
'I understand,' replied the pharmacist, 'it really would be a pity to waste such an expensive medication. Do you have a maid at all?'
The man said that he did.
'Well, why don't you occupy yourself with her?' inquired the pharmacist.

Naughty Stuff

The bloke snorted, 'I don't *need* to take Viagra when I'm with the maid!'

★ ★ ★

Blake and Eddy had just finished training on the footy oval and headed for the bathrooms to shower. As they are getting dressed, Blake reaches into his locker, pulls out a garter belt with some sexy black knickers and starts to put them on.
'Hey, Blake,' said Eddy, astonished, 'how long have you been wearing those things?'
Blake replied, 'Ever since my wife found them in the glove compartment of my car.'

★ ★ ★

More Great Kiwi Jokes

Jack decided to go skiing with his buddy, Tim. They loaded up Jack's minivan and headed to Queenstown. After driving for a short while, they got caught in a terrible blizzard. They pulled into a nearby farm and asked the attractive lady who answered the door if they could spend the night.

'I realise it's terrible weather out there and I have this huge house all to myself, but I'm recently widowed,' she explained, 'and I'm afraid the neighbours will talk if I let you stay in my house.'

'Not to worry,' Jack said. 'We'll be happy to sleep in the barn, and if the weather improves enough to drive safely, we'll be gone at first light.'

The lady agreed and the two men found their way to the barn and settled in for the night. Come morning, the weather had cleared and they got on their way and enjoyed a great weekend of skiing.

About nine months later, Jack got an unexpected letter from an attorney. It took him a few minutes to figure it out, but he finally determined that it was from the lawyer of that attractive widow he met near Queenstown. He dropped in on his friend Tim and asked, 'Tim, do you remember that good-looking widow from the farm we stayed at on our ski holiday?'

Naughty Stuff

'Yes, I do.'
'Did you happen to get up in the middle of the night, go to the house and fool around with her?'
'Yes,' Tim replied, a little embarrassed about being found out. 'I have to admit that I did.'
'And did you happen to use my name instead of telling her your name?'
Tim's face turned red and he said, 'Yeah, sorry buddy, I'm afraid I did. Why do you ask?'
'No need to apologise, Timbo - she just died and left me everything!'

★ ★ ★

Oddities

Once upon a time there lived a king. As is the case with all kings, he had a beautiful daughter, Princess Penelope. But there was a problem. Everything the princess touched would melt. No matter what: metal, wood, stone, anything she touched would melt. Because of this, men were afraid of her. Nobody would dare marry her. The king despaired: what could he do to help his daughter? He consulted his wizards and magicians. One wizard told the king, 'If your daughter touches just one thing that does not melt in her hands, she will be cured.' The king was overjoyed and came up with a plan. The next day, he announced a royal competition. Any man that could bring his daughter an object that wouldn't melt when she touched it

Oddities

would marry her and inherit the king's wealth. Three young princes took up the challenge. The first prince brought a sword of the finest steel. But alas, once the princess touched it, it melted. The prince went away sadly. The second prince brought diamonds. He thought diamonds were the hardest substance in the world and would not melt. But alas, once the princess touched them, they melted. He, too, was sent away, very disappointed. The third prince approached. He told the princess, 'Put your hand in my pocket and feel what is in there.' The princess did as she was told, though she turned red. She felt something hard. She held it in her hand. And it did not melt!

The king was overjoyed. Everybody in the kingdom was overjoyed. And the third prince married the princess and they both lived happily ever after.

Question: What was in the prince's pants?
Answer: M&Ms, of course. They melt in your mouth, not in your hand.

★ ★ ★

A man walks into a bar holding a newt. 'A jug of Lion Red for me,' he says to the bartender, 'and a shandy for my pet, Tiny, here.'
The bartender frowns at the man, puzzled, 'Of

all things, why did you call him "Tiny"?'
'Well,' says the man, 'he is my newt.'

★ ★ ★

Ray loses his wife Jane in a freak scuba-diving accident, and the police are unable to recover the body. Some days later, Ray gets a knock at his door and is greeted by two solemn police officers.
'We've found your wife, but we have some bad news, some good news, and some really great news. Which news do you want to hear first?' says the first officer.
Ray chooses the bad news first, so the cop explains, 'Well, we found your wife's body at the bottom of Rosalie Bay.'
'Oh my God,' says Ray, reeling. 'What could possibly be the good news?'
'Well,' says the second policeman, 'when we pulled her up she had two five-kilo crayfish and a dozen good-sized crabs on her.'
'My Lord!' shrieks Ray in disbelief, 'If that's the good news, what's the great news?'
The first cop smiles, 'We're going to pull her up again tomorrow.'

★ ★ ★

Oddities

A kindergarten teacher was telling the story of *The Three Little Pigs* to her class. 'So,' said the teacher, 'the first pig went to find straw to build his house so that the big, bad wolf could not huff and puff it down. He saw a farmer wheeling a wheelbarrow full of straw and he said to the farmer, "Please, Mr Farmer, can I buy some straw from you so I can build a house to protect me from the big, bad wolf?" And what do you think the farmer said?' the teacher asked her students.

At that point, little Jamie's hand rose from the back of the class, waving excitedly. 'Yes, Jamie? What do you think the farmer said?' the teacher asked.

Jamie exclaimed, 'Holy crap - a talking pig!'

★ ★ ★

A guy walks into a chemist and asks for a bottle of Viagra. The chemist eyes him suspiciously and asks, 'Do you have a prescription for that?'
'No,' says the guy shaking his head, 'but will this photo of my wife do?'

★ ★ ★

Jeremy was hired to play his saxophone on the score of a new movie and he was really excited because he had two long solos. After the sessions, he wanted to see the finished product, so asked the producer where he could catch the film. The producer was a bit embarrassed to admit to Jeremy at this stage that it was actually a porno movie he'd played

Oddities

music for, but told him where it was screening.

Jeremy, a pretty open-minded guy, went to the cinema and sat in the back row beside an elderly couple. The movie started and it soon proved to be the filthiest, most perverted porno flick he'd ever seen. Embarrassed, he turned to the elderly couple beside him and whispered, 'I'm only here for the music.'

The woman turned to Jeremy and whispered back, 'That's okay, we're just here to see our daughter.'

★ ★ ★

Rangi said to his mate, 'My grandpa doesn't drink, smoke, gamble, eat fatty foods or even swear. We're all going to celebrate his ninety-fifth birthday tomorrow down at the marae!'

Hiwi looked at him smirking, and asked, 'How?'

★ ★ ★

'How long have you been working here?' one employee said to another.

The other answered, 'Ever since the boss threatened to fire me.'

★ ★ ★

If gay men come out of the closet, what do lesbians come out of?
The liquor cabinet.

★ ★ ★

A big Texan cowboy stopped at a local restaurant following a day of drinking and roaming around in Mexico. While sipping his tequila, he noticed a sizzling, scrumptious-looking platter being served at the next table. Not only did it look good, the smell was wonderful.
He asked the waiter, 'What is that you just served? It smells delicious!'
The waiter replied, 'Ah, you have excellent taste! Those are bull's testicles from the bullfight this morning. A true delicacy!'
The cowboy, blanching a little at first, replied, 'Well, what the heck, I'm on holiday – I should live a little! Waiter, bring me some!'
The waiter replied, 'I am so sorry. We can only serve one pair of testicles per day because there is only one bullfight each morning. Why don't you come in early tomorrow and place your order, and you will be able to try some testicles then.'
The next morning, the cowboy returned, placed his order, and then that evening he was served the one and only special delicacy

Oddities

of the day. After a few bites, and inspecting the contents of his plate, he called to the waiter and said, 'These are truly superb, but why is it that they are much, much smaller than the ones I saw you serve yesterday?' The waiter shrugged his shoulders and replied, 'Ah, mister, sometimes the bull wins.'

★ ★ ★

The tomcat, on the prowl as usual, spotted a gorgeous kitten on the other side of the fence. He decided to try to visit her. He gave a mighty leap and landed on the other side. The gorgeous kitten was impressed with the tomcat's big leap, and sauntered over. 'Wow,' she cooed. 'That was amazing. Do you want to go somewhere and get intimate?' 'Erm, afraid not,' said the tomcat, looking pained. 'The fence was higher than I thought.'

★ ★ ★

Rangi joined the army to get a bit of travel and ended up in East Timor in the paratroop regiment as an instructor. His first job was to take a group of Australian army recruits on their first jump from an aeroplane.
The next day, Dougie, a young Aussie, phones his father to tell him about his first day

paratrooping.

'So did you jump?' his dad asks.

'Well, we got up in the plane and this big Maori bloke opened the door and asked for volunteers. A dozen blokes got up and jumped.'

'Is that when you went?' asks his dad.

'Nah, not then,' says Dougie, 'the Maori started to grab the other blokes and throw them out the door.'

'So did you jump then?' asks his dad.

'Nah, not then,' says Dougie. 'Everyone else jumped, and I was the only one left. So I told the Maori bloke that I was too scared. He told me to get out of the plane or he would kick my arse.'

'So then did you jump?' asks his dad, exasperated.

'Nah, not then,' says Dougie. 'Eventually, this bloke pulled out a cricket bat and said, "Either you jump or I'm gonna stick this baby up your arse!".'

'So did you jump then, Dougie?' sighs his dad.

'Well, a little... at first.'

★ ★ ★

Prior to competing in the New Zealand Open, Tiger Woods is touring the North Island doing a spot of fishing. He needs petrol, so pulls

Oddities

into a service station near Taupo in his huge Mercedes.
'Howdy,' he says to the attendant, 'can you fill her up, please?'
As Tiger pulls out his car keys, two wooden tees fall out of his pocket.
'Bugger me!' marvels the attendant, 'what are they?'
Tiger looks down and smiles, 'Oh, they're just for putting my balls on when I'm driving.'
'Shit!' cries the attendant, 'Those blokes at Mercedes think of everything, don't they?'

★ ★ ★

When Adam walked into his local pub one night, the bartender noticed with great surprise that his head had shrunk to half its size. The bartender tried not to stare, but just couldn't help himself. 'I'm sorry to be so personal, mate,' he said to Adam, 'but what happened to you? Your head has shrunk!'
Adam nodded glumly. 'I was walking in the park the other day, when all of a sudden I came across a bottle with a strange cork in it. I took the cork out and there was this puff of pink smoke and out steps a genie. She was the most beautiful thing I'd ever seen. So when she tells me that she can grant me one wish, the first thing I ask is if she will go to

bed with me. "I'm sorry," she says, "but that's actually the one thing we genies aren't allowed to do." So I said, "Well, then, how about a little head?"

★ ★ ★

An Australian, a Kiwi and a South African are in a pub one night having a beer. All of a sudden the South African guzzles his beer, throws his glass in the air, pulls out a gun, shoots the glass to pieces and says, 'In South Africa our glasses are so cheap that we don't need to drink from the same one twice.'

Oddities

The Aussie, obviously impressed by this (simple things!) guzzles his beer, throws his glass into the air, pulls out his gun and shoots the glass to pieces and says, 'Well, mate, in Australia we have so much sand to make the glasses that we don't need to drink out of the same glass twice either.'
The Kiwi picks up his beer, guzzles it, throws his glass into the air, pulls out his gun, shoots the South African and the Aussie, and says, 'In New Zealand we have so many bloody South Africans and Aussies that we don't need to drink with the same ones twice.'

★ ★ ★

A woman rushes into the police station and cries, 'Help! I've been molested by a virgin!'
'By a virgin?' scoffs the desk sergeant, 'How do you know he was a virgin?
'Because I had to help him,' she gasps.

★ ★ ★

You Know You're Old When...
- Your little black book contains only next-of-kin.
- You get winded playing bridge.
- You're still chasing women but can't remember why.

- You turn out the lights for economic reasons.
- You sit in a rocking-chair but can't get it going.

★ ★ ★

'Have you got anything to say for yourself?' said the judge sternly after hearing the case.
'F- all,' muttered the defendant.
'What did he say?' asked the judge to the clerk. The clerk stood up, turned, and whispered quietly to the judge, 'He said "f- all", your worship.'
'That's funny,' said the judge, 'I'm sure I saw his lips move.'

★ ★ ★

Oddities

Fred visited the rubber factory in Dargaville one day. In the first room there was a loud sound of: Bang! Hiss! Bang! Hiss!
Fred turned to the foreman and asked, 'So what are you making in this room?'
The foreman replied, 'Teats for baby bottles. The "bang" makes the teat and the "hiss" puts a hole in the end.'
The next room was filled with different sounds: Bang! Bang! Bang! Bang! Hiss! Bang!
'And this is where we make the condoms,' explained the foreman.
'So why the "hiss" every now and then?' asked Fred.
'Well,' said the foreman, 'holes in condoms are good for the baby bottle business.'

★ ★ ★

How do you set up an Aussie in small business?
Set him up in a big business and wait.

★ ★ ★

A recent survey of Kiwi men showed that 10 per cent like women with thin legs and 15 per cent prefer women with muscular legs. The rest liked something in between.

★ ★ ★

A priest went fishing with a parishioner and he landed a massive fish. The parishioner bellowed, 'Man, that's a big f***er!'
'Language, please!' admonished the shocked priest.
To cover up his mistake, the parishioner replied, 'Oh, no, Father! You misunderstood, you see that's a type of fish, a f***er, and it's a mighty big one!'
Back at the parish, the priest proudly told the Archbishop that he had caught a f***er, and that it was in the fridge.
The Archbishop was furious, 'Father! You wash your filthy mouth out!'
'No, no! That's what sort of fish it is - a f***er,' laughed the priest.
'Oh, then why don't I gut the f***er and we

can have it for dinner,' replied the Archbishop.
In the kitchen, Mother Superior asked the
Archbishop what he was doing.'
'Oh, I'm just cleaning this f***er,' explained the
Archbishop.
Mother Superior was shocked, 'Language,
please!' she chided.
'No, no, Mother,' laughed the Archbishop,
'that's the sort of fish it is - it's called a f***er!'
'Oh, very well then,' beamed the nun, 'let me
cook it for you.'
The Pope (who just happened to have
stopped by) was served the fish for dinner. He
took one bite and exclaimed, 'Why, that's
delicious!'
'I caught the f***er!' smiled the priest.
'I gutted the f***er!' laughed the Archbishop.
'And I cooked the f***er!' hooted the Mother
Superior.
The Pope sat in silence, gulped his wine, lit a
cigar, and slowly laughed, 'You know, what? I
think you bastards are alright!'

★ ★ ★

Bruce was at the pub one night, downing a
few, when he noticed the guy next to him
slide off his seat and land on the floor. Being
good at heart, Bruce decides to help the guy
home. He manages to get the guy's address

from the bartender, puts his arm around the guy's waist and struggles to get him out the door. No sooner do they hit the street, when the man's legs crumple beneath him and he falls into a gutter. Bruce helps him up, and once again the man falls over. Bruce is getting a bit annoyed now and says to the semi-conscious man, 'Jesus, mate, surely at your age you should know when to stop drinking!' After a couple more attempts at getting the guy to stand up, Bruce gives up and throws the guy over his shoulder.

When he reaches the man's house, he knocks grumpily on the door and says to the woman who answers, 'Here's your husband. If I were you I'd have a bit of a chat with him about his drinking problem.'

'I will,' she promises. 'But tell me, where's his wheelchair?'

★ ★ ★

Little Billie was a very bad boy who wanted a bike more than anything else in the world. His mother said he could only have one if he started behaving himself, which he promised to do. He tried as hard as he could, but his naughty habits were well entrenched and he kept getting into trouble. His mother could see that he was trying to be good, so she

Oddities

suggested that he write a letter to Jesus as it might make it easier for him to behave.
Little Billie went to his room and began to write a letter. 'Dear Jesus,' he began, 'I promise to behave for the rest of my life if you give me a bike.'
Realising that he couldn't keep this promise, he started again. 'Dear Jesus, if you give me a bike, I'll be good for a month.'
Thinking for a second, he realised that even this promise would be broken, so he screwed the paper up.
Running into his parents' bedroom, he removed his mum's statue of the Holy Mother, put it in a shoebox, and hid it in his desk drawer. He started on a new sheet of paper. 'Dear Jesus,' he wrote, 'if you ever want to see your mother again...'

★ ★ ★

Out on the beat one night, a policeman came across a bruised and bloodied young man on the footpath. 'Sir, what happened? Can you describe the person who beat you up?'
'Of course,' said the man, spitting out a few teeth. 'In fact, that's just what I was doing when the ugly son of a bitch slugged me.'

★ ★ ★

The Whites had recently moved into a brand new home in a new suburb, and were having a housewarming party. One of the guests asked Brigitte how she liked the new house. 'It's great,' she said. 'I have my own room, Sally has her own room, and Tamara has her own room, too. But poor Mum is still in with Dad.'

★★★

The solicitor strode over to the witness stand. 'Come now, Mr Brock. It was after midnight, yet you say you saw my client murder Mr Crepney from nearly six blocks away. Just how far can you see at night?'
Mr Brock shrugged. 'Well, I dunno. How far away is the moon?'

★★★

At the cinema, an usher noticed a man stretched across four seats. 'I'm sorry, sir, but you're only allowed to have one seat.' But the man didn't budge.
The usher tried again. 'Sir, if you don't move, I'll have to get the manager.' But again, the man didn't budge.
Furious, the usher went to get the manager, who similarly was not able to get the man to

Oddities

move. He had no choice but to call the police. A policeman arrived in no time and looked down at the guy, still stretched across four seats.
'What's yer name, bud?'
The man mumbled, 'Paul.'
'And where are you from, Paul?'
'The balcony.'

★ ★ ★

Advantages of Being Fat

1. Your gut acts as convenient TV tray for nachos.
2. Your partner doesn't have to worry about you running off with someone sexy.
3. You get more value for money – more material in that shirt for the same price.
4. It's a great way to meet cute female cardiologists.
5. Extra gravity makes it that much less likely you'll ever be thrown free of the Earth into deep space.
6. You feel like you can get your money's worth at All You Can Eat buffets.
7. Your bellybutton can store up to two dollars in change for the parking meter.
8. You can eat as much chocolate as you want. Hell, why not? It's not like you're scared of getting fat.

★ ★ ★

What does an Aussie blonde say after multiple orgasms?
Well done, team.

★ ★ ★

Oddities

What's the definition of safe sex in Australia?
Branding the sheep that kick.

★ ★ ★

Two drovers were checking fences on a big sheep station south of Darwin. They came across a sheep with its head caught in a fence. One drover dismounts, drops his pants and starts screwing the sheep.
He turns to the other drover and says, 'Your turn, mate.'
The other bloke replies, 'I don't think my head will fit between the wires.'

★ ★ ★

What do you do if a rottweiler humps your leg?
Fake an orgasm.

★ ★ ★

The deaf mute needed more condoms and nervously approached the chemist. He opened his fly, put his penis on the counter, pointed to it and laid down a $10 bill.
With an understanding nod, the pharmacist took his own penis out, laid it on the counter beside the other man's, grinned in triumph, grabbed the money and walked away.

★ ★ ★

In the outback, 'Tie Me Kangaroo Down, Sport' is considered the drover's love song.

★ ★ ★

The owners of a Chinese takeaway are in bed.
'I want a sixty-nine right now!' demands the husband.
'What?' replies his wife sleepily, 'you want a sweet and sour pork right now?'

★ ★ ★

You Must Be Italian If...
1. You have to shave twice a day, yet still you cry when your mother yells at you.
2. Your mechanic, plumber, electrician, accountant, and travel agent are all blood relatives.

Oddities

3. Your two best friends are your cousin and your brother-in-law's brother-in-law.
4. You are a card-carrying VIP at more than three after-hours clubs.
5. You have at least five cousins living in the same street. All five of those cousins are named after your grandfather or grandmother.
6. You are on a first-name basis with at least seven banquet hall owners
7. You netted more than $50,000 on your first communion.
8. You 'speaka' with an accent when you're with your family and friends, but sound completely normal when with non-Italians.

The 10 Benefits of Being Old
1. People call at 9 p.m. and ask, 'Did I wake you?'
2. No one expects you to run into a burning building.
3. People no longer view you as a hypochondriac – just old.
4. Things you buy now won't wear out.
5. You don't have to worry about saving 'for the future'.
6. You can avoid crowds at restaurants by eating dinner at 5 p.m.
7. You enjoy hearing about other people's operations.

More Great Kiwi Jokes

8. You have a party and the neighbours don't even realise it.
9. Your investment in health insurance is finally beginning to pay off.
10. Your secrets are safe with your friends because they can't remember them either.

★ ★ ★

How many civil servants does it take to change a light bulb?
Forty. One to change it, and thirty-nine to do the paperwork.

★ ★ ★

How many elephants does it take to change a light bulb?
Two, but it has to be a pretty big light bulb.

★ ★ ★

How many musicians does it take to change a light bulb?
Five. One to change the bulb and four to get in free because they know the guy who owns the socket.

★ ★ ★

Oddities

A big Maori bloke from Otara gets accepted into King's College. On the first day at school he gets lost, so approaches another student for directions.
'Yo, bro, where's the library at?'
'Just a moment, my dear chap,' says the other student. 'Here at King's we never end a sentence with a preposition.'
'Okay. So where's the library at, motherf***er?'

★ ★ ★

How many possums does it take to change a light bulb?
Two. One to change it and the other to watch out for traffic.

★ ★ ★

What do you say to a blonde who won't have sex with you?
Want another beer?

★ ★ ★

'Doctor, doctor! Can I get pregnant from anal intercourse?' she asked.
'Absolutely,' replied the doctor, 'where do you think lawyers come from.'

★ ★ ★

After having blood tests, the doctor called Hemi into his office.
'There's a problem, Hemi,' sighed the doctor. 'Your wife either has Alzheimer's or AIDS.'
'What the Hell should I do?' cried Hemi.
'Drive her about five kilometres from home and drop her off. If she finds her way back, for God's sake, don't have sex.'

★ ★ ★

Oddities

At the end of a job interview, the managing director asked the young candidate, who was fresh out of university, what he wanted as his starting salary. The graduate said, 'Well, I think $120,000 a year would be appropriate, depending on what the package contained.'
The managing director said, 'Well, what would you say to nine weeks of annual leave, three paid overseas holidays a year, long service leave after five years, and a new Porsche every two years?'
The candidate sat up straight, eyes shining, and said, 'Wow! Are you kidding?'
The managing director said, 'Yes, but you started it.'

★ ★ ★

Doctor Ted was very depressed. He'd been caught in bed with a patient. He was so worried that he confided in a friend.
'You worry too much, Ted,' laughed his mate. 'You aren't the first doctor to sleep with a patient, and you certainly won't be the last.'
'I know that,' replied Ted, 'but I won't be considered the city's top vet anymore, will I?'

★ ★ ★

A man walked up to a little old lady rocking in a chair on her porch.
'I couldn't help noticing how happy you look,' he said. 'What's your secret for a long, happy life?'
'I smoke three packs of cigarettes a day,' she said. 'I also do a bit of smack every day, drink a case of vodka every week, eat chocolate with every meal, and never, ever exercise,' she said proudly.
'That's amazing,' said the man. 'How old are you?'
'Twenty-four.'

★ ★ ★

What does daylight saving time mean in Wellington?
An extra hour of wind.

★ ★ ★

A grasshopper walks into a bar, pulls up a stool and orders a beer. The barman pours the beer and says, 'Do you know we have a drink named after you?' To which the grasshopper replies, 'Really? You have a drink called Bob?'

★ ★ ★

Oddities

A man was visiting his wife who was in a coma in hospital. He touched her left breast and noticed that she sighed. He immediately summoned the doctor. The doctor told him to touch her right breast, and this time she let out a little moan. The doctor then suggested he try oral sex to test her responses, and that he'd come back in fifteen minutes to check on them.
On his return he found the woman near death.
'What the Hell happened?' he asked.
'I think she might have choked.'

★ ★ ★

Actual Notes Found on Medical Charts
1. The patient has no rigours or shaking chills, but her husband states she was very hot in bed last night.
2. The patient has chest pain if she lies on her left side for over a year.
3. On the second day the knee was better, and on the third day it disappeared.
4. The patient is tearful and crying constantly. She also appears to be sad.
5. Discharge status: alive, but without my permission.
6. Healthy-appearing decrepit 70-year-old male, mentally eight years. The patient refused an autopsy.

7. The patient has no previous history of suicides.
8. The patient has left white blood cells at another hospital.
9. The patient's medical history has been remarkably insignificant with only an 80-kilogram weight gain in the past three days.
10. The patient had waffles for breakfast and anorexia for lunch.
11. The patient is numb from her toes down.
12. While in ER, she was examined, x-rated and sent home.
13. The skin was moist and dry.
14. Occasional, constant infrequent headaches.
15. Patient was alert and unresponsive.
16. Rectal examination revealed a normal size thyroid.
17. The patient stated that she had been constipated for most of her life, until she got a divorce.
18. Both breasts are equal and reactive to light and accommodation.
19. Examination of genitalia reveals that he is circus sized.
20. The lab test indicated abnormal lover function.
21. The patient was to have a bowel resection. However, he took a job as a lawyer instead.

Oddities

22. The pelvic exam will be done later on the floor.
23. The patient was seen in consultation with Dr Cody, who felt we should sit on the abdomen and I agree.
24. The patient has two teenage children, but no other abnormalities.

★ ★ ★

A philosophy professor stood before his class and had some items in front of him. When the class began, wordlessly, he picked up a large empty mayonnaise jar and began filling it with rocks that were about five centimetres in diameter. He then asked the students if the jar was full, and they all agreed it was. So the professor then picked up a box of pebbles and poured them into the jar. He shook the jar lightly. The pebbles, of course, rolled into the open areas between the rocks. He then asked the students again if the jar was full. They agreed it was. The professor picked up a box of sand and poured it into the jar. Of course, the sand filled up everything else.

'Now,' said the professor, 'I want you to recognise that this is our life. The rocks are the important things – your family, your partner, your health, your children, your friends – things that if everything else was lost and only they remained, your life would still be full. The pebbles are the other things that matter, like your job, your house, your car. The sand is everything else. The small stuff. If you put the sand into the jar first, there is no room for the pebbles or the rocks. The same goes for your life. If you spend all your time and energy on the small stuff, you will never have room for the things that really matter. Pay attention to the things that are critical to your happiness. Play with your children. Take time to get medical checkups. Take your partner out dancing. There will always be time to go to work, clean the house, give a dinner party and fix the guttering. Just remember to take care of the rocks first, the things that really matter. Get your priorities right. The rest is just sand.'

The students were all duly impressed with the professor's philosophy, and sat open-mouthed listening to him.

Suddenly, a student then took the jar that the other students and the professor agreed was full, and proceeded to pour in a glass of beer. Of course the beer filled the remaining spaces within the jar, so that now the jar was really full.

The moral of this story? No matter how full your life is, there is always room for beer.

★ ★ ★

Oddities

Warning: Work Virus

There is a new virus going around called 'Work'. If you receive any sort of 'Work' at all, whether via email or over the internet, or simply handed to you by a co-worker, DO NOT OPEN IT. This vicious virus has been circulating around our building for months. Those who have been tempted to open 'Work' have found that their social life is deleted and their taste for alcohol disappears. If you do encounter 'Work' via email or are faced with any 'Work' at all, to purge the virus, send an email to your boss with the words 'I've had enough of your garbage... I'm off to the pub.' The 'Work' should automatically be forgotten by your brain and will not re-infect you. If you receive 'Work' in paper form, simply lift the document and drag it to your rubbish bin. Go to the nearest pub with two friends and order three rounds of beer. After repeating this action 14 times, you will find that 'Work' will no longer be of any relevance to you. Send this message to everyone in your address book. If you do NOT have anyone in your address book, then I'm afraid the 'Work' virus has already corrupted your life.

★ ★ ★

More Great Kiwi Jokes

A man walks into a doctor's surgery, obviously in a lot of pain.
'Doc!' he gasps, 'You've got to help me. I've got a cricket bat stuck up my arse!'
'How's that?' asks the doctor.
'Don't bloody start that,' growls the man.

★ ★ ★

A man sees an ad in the paper for a talking dingo selling at just $20. He decides to go and check it out. He rocks up to the address and says to the dingo standing at the gate, 'Are you the talking dog, mate?'

Oddities

The dingo replies, 'Why, yes, indeed I am!'
'Wow, that's amazing! What else can you do?' says the bloke.
'Well, I wrote a column for the Sydney Morning Herald, I've swum the Tasman, and last year I played bass guitar at all of Rod Stewart's comeback concerts. What's more, I've just been selected to play half-back for the Wallabies.'
Astonished, the bloke turns to the dingo's owner who's lurking in the driveway and says, 'Mate! Why are you selling this amazing dog for only $20.'
The owner shakes his head despairingly, 'I can't stand his bloody lies.'

★ ★ ★

Late one evening, a couple of Maori blokes are leaving the beach with two buckets of fish when they are stopped by a fisheries inspector. 'Those fish look under-size to me. You fellas could be in for a big fine, you know,' says the inspector sternly.
The men smile, 'No, you're misunderstood, sir. You see, we haven't been fishing - these here are our pet fish. Every night we take them down to the beach for a swim. When we whistle they jump back in the bucket and we take them home.'

'Bullshit!' frowns the inspector. 'This I've got to see.'
'Okay,' smiles one of the Maoris, and he proceeds down the beach emptying both buckets of fish into the water. The threesome all watch for a few minutes until the inspector gets annoyed.
'So when are you going to whistle them back in?' he snaps.
'Whistle who back in?'
'The fish of course!' he seethes.
'Fish?' say the blokes in unison, 'What bloody fish?'

★ ★ ★

A Dictionary of Body Parts
Artery = The study of paintings
Bacteria = Back door to cafeteria
Barium = What doctors do when patients die
Caesarean section = A neighbourhood in Rome
Cauterise = Made eye contact with her
Dilate = To live long
Enema = Not a friend
Fibula = A small lie
Genital = Non-Jewish person
Hangnail = What you hang your coat on
Herpes = Famous Greek philosopher
Impotent = Distinguished, well known

Oddities

Labour pain = Getting hurt at work
Morbid = A higher offer than I bid
Nitrates = Cheaper than day rates
Node = I knew it
Outpatient = A person who has fainted
Pap smear = A fatherhood test
Pelvis = Brother to Elvis
Protein = In favour of young people
Recovery room = Place to do upholstery
Rectum = Damn near killed him
Secretion = Hiding something
Terminal illness = Getting sick at the airport
Tibia = Country in northern Africa
Tumour = More than one
Urine = Opposite of you're out
Varicose = Near by

★ ★ ★

What's the definition of gross ignorance?
144 blondes.

★ ★ ★

How do you keep a girl from having sex?
Marry her.

★ ★ ★

Why do blondes like cars with sun roofs?
More leg room.

★ ★ ★

If a woman with briefs is a lawyer, what is a woman without briefs?
A solicitor.

★ ★ ★

What is an Aussie sheila's favourite nursery rhyme?
Humpme Dumpme.

★ ★ ★

Oddities

What's the difference between a woman with PMT and the KBG?
You can reason with the KGB.

★ ★ ★

One day, in line at the company cafeteria, Jack says to Mike behind him, 'My elbow hurts like Hell. I guess I'd better see a doctor.'
'Listen, you don't have to bother doing that,' Mike replies. 'There's a diagnostic computer at the chemist around the corner. Just give it a urine sample and then the computer'll tell you what's wrong with you and what to do about it. It takes ten seconds and costs five bucks - a Hell of a lot cheaper and quicker than a doctor.'
So Jack deposits a urine sample in an old Vegemite jar and takes it to the chemist. He deposits five dollars and the computer lights up and asks for the urine sample. He pours the sample into the slot and waits. Ten seconds later, the computer spits out a printout: 'You have tennis elbow. Soak your arm in warm water and avoid heavy activity; it will improve in two weeks.'
That evening while Jack was thinking about how amazing the new technology was, he began wondering if the computer could be fooled. He mixed some tap water, a stool

sample from the dog, urine samples from his wife and daughter and masturbated into the mixture for good measure.

The next day, Jack hurries back to the chemist eager to check the results. He deposits another five dollars, pours in his concoction and waits for the results. The computer prints out the following:

1. Your tap water is too hard. Get a water softener.
2. Your dog has ringworm. Bathe him with anti-fungal shampoo.
3. Your daughter has a cocaine habit. Get her into rehab.
4. Your wife is pregnant with twin boys. They aren't yours. Get a lawyer.
5. If you don't stop playing with yourself, your elbow will never get better.'

★ ★ ★

Letters of Recommendation for Employees
For the chronically absent:
'A man like him is hard to find.'
'It seemed his career was just taking off.'

For the office drunk:
'I feel his real talent is wasted here.'
'We generally found him loaded with work to do.'

Oddities

For an employee with no ambition:
'He could not care less about the number of hours he had to put in.'
'You would indeed be fortunate to get this person to work for you.'
'He consistently achieves the standards he sets for himself.'

For an employee who is so unproductive that the job is better left unfilled:
'I can assure you that no person would be better for the job.'

For an employee who is not worth further consideration as a job candidate:
'I would urge you to waste no time in making this candidate an offer of employment.'
'All in all, I cannot say enough good things about this candidate or recommend him too highly.'

★ ★ ★

One day a ten-year-old boy was walking down the street when a car pulled up beside him and wound down its window. 'I'll give you a bag of lollies if you get in the car,' said the driver.
'No way, get stuffed!' replied the boy.
'How about a bag of lollies and ten dollars?' the driver asked.

'I said "no way",' replied the boy.
'What about a bag of lollies and fifty dollars?' asked the driver.
'No, I'm not getting in the car,' answered the boy.
'Okay, I'll give you a bag of lollies and $100,' the driver offered.
'No!' replied the boy.
'What will it take to get you in the car?' asked the driver.
The boy replied, 'Listen Dad, you bought the bloody Hyundai Excel, you live with it!'

★ ★ ★

Miss Susie was conducting an English lesson for her junior class. 'Class,' she said, I'm going to give you a word, and I'd like one of you to say a sentence using that word. Would any of you like to give me a sentence using the word "lovely"?'
Cara put up her hand.
'Yes, Cara, go ahead,' prompted Miss Susie.
'Yesterday I went swimming in the lake. The sky was blue and the grass was green and the weather was lovely.'
'Very good, Cara,' said Miss Susie. 'I think I'll make it a little harder now. Can anybody give me a sentence with the word 'lovely' in it twice?'

Oddities

Little Bobby in the back row raised his hand.
'Okay, Bobby, go ahead,' said the teacher.
'Last night,' began little Bobby, 'my fifteen-year-old sister went into our parents' bedroom and said, "Mum and Dad, I'm pregnant." Dad said, "Oh, lovely, that's f***ing lovely!".'

★ ★ ★

Anne was a single mother who had two teenage sons, and over coffee with her friend one day she confided that she was having a real problem with the foul language her sons used all the time. Her friend told her, 'Listen, I had the same problem with my two terrors, and I discovered that the best way to deal with it was, believe it or not, to use physical violence. When one of them says something that offends you, just reach across and give him a good slap across his ear and say you will not put up with their foul language. It really works.'
Anne decided to try it. The next morning she was in the kitchen when the two boys came down for breakfast. She asked the first boy what he wanted to eat.
'Give me some f***ing porridge,' he said. Anne immediately reached across the table and gave him a hard slap across his ear that knocked him right out of his chair.

She then turned to her other son and said, 'And darling, what would you like for breakfast?'
'Well,' he answered, 'you can bet your sweet arse I'm not having any of that f***ing porridge!'

★ ★ ★

Scott and Mel go fishing one Saturday, and even though they are at it from dawn to dusk, they only catch one fish each. As one fish wouldn't make a very substantial meal, they start arguing between them as to who should take home both fish.
Mel said, 'I know a good way to decide. One of us will get to kick the other guy in the balls as hard as he can. Then that guy will get a chance to kick the other guy in the balls as hard as he can. When one of us says, "Stop" the other guy will get to keep the fish.'
'That sounds fair,' said Scott. 'Which one of us should go first?'
'Well, seeing as it was my idea in the first place, I believe I should be the one to go first.'
'Fair enough,' replied Scott. With that Mel kicked him in the balls as hard as he could. Scott fell to the ground clutching his groin and screaming in agony.

Oddities

A few minutes later he managed to stand up, and was about to return the kick when Mel said, 'Aw, never mind, Scotty mate, you can keep the fish.'

★ ★ ★

A strong young man at the construction site was bragging that he could outdo anyone in a feat of strength. He made a special case of making fun of Morris, one of the older workmen. After several minutes, Morris had enough.
'Why don't you put your money where your mouth is?' he said. 'I will bet a week's wages that I can haul something in a wheelbarrow over to that building that you won't be able to wheel back.'
'You're on, old man,' the young bloke replied. 'It's a bet! Let's see what you've got.'
Morris reached out and grabbed the wheelbarrow by the handles. Then, nodding to the young fella, he said, 'All right. Get in.'

★ ★ ★

Why Dogs Are Better Than Kids

1. It doesn't take an hour to get a dog ready to go outside in the winter.
2. Dogs don't lie.
3. Dogs never resist nap-time.
4. You don't need to get extra phone lines for a dog.
5. Dogs don't care if the peas have been touched by the mashed potatoes.
6. Dogs are housebroken by the time they are twelve weeks old.
7. Your dog is not embarrassed to be seen with you on the street.

Oddities

8. If your dog is a bad seed, your genes cannot be blamed.

★ ★ ★

When the office printer's type began to grow faint, the office manager called a local repair shop where a friendly man informed him that the printer probably needed to be cleaned. Because the store charged $50 for such cleanings, he said, the manager might try reading the printer's manual and doing the job himself.
Pleasantly surprised by his honesty, the office manager asked, 'Does your boss know that you discourage business?'
'Actually, it's my boss's idea,' the employee replied. 'We usually make more money on repairs if we let people try to fix things themselves first.'

★ ★ ★

A young athlete was doing push-ups in the park when a drunk staggered past, and then came back and laughed at him.
'What's so funny,' said the athlete indignantly.
'I hate to tell you this,' slurred the drunk, 'but your girlfriend's gone home!'

★ ★ ★

What do you call a blonde at university?
A visitor.

★ ★ ★

Three old women were sitting on a park bench when a man came by and flashed at them. Two of them had a stroke, but the third wasn't fast enough.

★ ★ ★

What's the definition of safe sex?
Masturbation.

★ ★ ★

Women Through the Ages
16-25: like Africa - partly explored, partly virgin territory.
25-35: like the Far East - hot and mysterious.
35-45: like America - willing to experiment, but partly plastic.
55-65: like Russia - seen better days.
65+: like Antarctica - everyone knows where it is, but no one wants to go there.

★ ★ ★

Oddities

Two uni students get busted for possession of drugs and appear in court the next day. After reading the charges, the judge throws his arms up in despair, saying, 'I can't believe the drug epidemic we have these days. I'm so busy with drug cases I can't even hear your case for ten days. Look, I tell you what. You two are young; you've got your careers ahead of you. As this is your first offence, I'm willing to give you a break. If each of you can get ten of your fellow students to sign a pledge vowing to give up drugs for life, I'll let you off with a warning.'

The two frightened students agreed to try to get the pledges.

Ten days later they were back in court before the judge. The judge said to the first one, 'Well, tell me, did you manage to get some students to vow to stay off drugs?'

'Yes, your honour, I did,' the student replied.

'Good, good,' said the judge. 'And just how many did you get?'

'Ten,' said the student.

'Excellent. How did you get them to sign?'

'Well, your honour,' began the student, 'I took a small pad of paper and on it I drew a dot and a circle. I then pointed to the dot and told them that was the size of one's brain when one is on drugs. I then pointed at the circle and said, "And this is the size of one's brain when one is not on drugs!" My friends were so impressed they agreed to vow to stay off drugs.'

'Fantastic,' said the judge. 'You may go; you've earned yourself a reprieve.'

Turning to the second student, he asked, 'Now, young man, did you collect pledges too?'

The student said proudly, 'You betcha. I got ninety-eight people to sign a pledge.'

'That's astonishing!' exclaimed the judge. 'How on Earth did you manage to do that?'

'Well, your honour, it was easy. I took a small pad of paper. On it I drew a dot and a circle. Then I pointed at the dot and told everyone that this dot represents the size of your arsehole, before you go to prison...'

★ ★ ★

A travelling salesman finds himself stranded out in Hicksville. He wearily walks to a nearby farmhouse, whereupon the farmer offers to let him share the guest room with another guest, a 'little redheaded schoolteacher'.

'Oh, terrific,' said the salesman. 'And don't you worry, I'll be a real gentleman.'

'Yeah?' replied the farmer. 'Well, so will the little redheaded schoolteacher.'

★ ★ ★

Oddities

Lenny and Eira, two five-year-old Jewish kids, are walking home after school one day. Lenny says, 'Boy, I'm really scared about tomorrow.'
Eira replies, 'Why?'
Lenny says, 'Well, I'm going to be circumcised and I hear it's really painful.'
Eira says, 'Boy, you got that right. I was circumcised when I was born and I couldn't walk for a year.'

★ ★ ★

More Great Kiwi Jokes

Mandy is in a hotel and calls the manager with a complaint. 'My whole bed shakes every time those darned trains go by,' she said. The hotel manager goes up to her room to investigate.
'The vibration practically shakes me out of the bed,' Mandy said to him. 'You can't really feel it if you're not lying down. Why don't you get under the covers and see for yourself?'
The manager lay down on the bed, just as Mandy's husband walked into the room. 'What the Hell do you think you are doing?' the husband demanded.
The manager replied, 'Would you believe, I'm waiting for a train?'

★ ★ ★

A bloke is standing in line at the theatre waiting to buy a ticket. Suddenly he feels these two manly hands on his shoulders, and they begin to massage him. He turns around and says to the guy behind him, 'What the Hell do you think you're doing?'
The guy behind him says, 'Oh, I'm sorry. I'm a sports masseuse and I do this out of force of habit. Please pardon my behaviour.'
The bloke replies, 'Don't give me that crap! I'm a lawyer and you don't see me trying to screw the guy in front of me do you?'

★ ★ ★

Oddities

You Know You've Reached Middle Age When...

1. You go to the doctor and you realise you are now so old, you have to pay someone to look at you naked.
2. You stand in front of a mirror and can see your butt without turning around.
3. You go in for your annual mammogram and realise it is the only time someone will ask you to appear topless in film.
4. You look at your gum-popping, mobile-toting, know-it-all teenager and think, 'I gave myself stretch marks for this?'
5. You notice you no longer have upper arms, just wingspans.
6. Your memory really starts to go. The only thing you still retain is water.
7. You get all excited if a guy on a construction site whistles at you.
8. If someone bumps into you and says, 'Ooops, sorry Miss,' it makes your day.

★ ★ ★

How is the census taken in Israel?
They roll a coin down the street.

★ ★ ★

A man had been stung on the penis by a bee. His wife sent him to the doctor with a note: *'Dear Doctor, please take out the sting, but leave the swelling in.'*

★ ★ ★

What's the correct term for when an Aussie's girlfriend has an orgasm?
A miracle.

★ ★ ★

What do you call an Aussie with two sheep?
Lucky.

★ ★ ★

What do you call an Aussie with three sheep?
A pimp.

★ ★ ★

What's a sure sign that a man is going to be unfaithful?
He has a penis.

★ ★ ★

Oddities

What's got four legs and an arm?
A happy pit-bull.

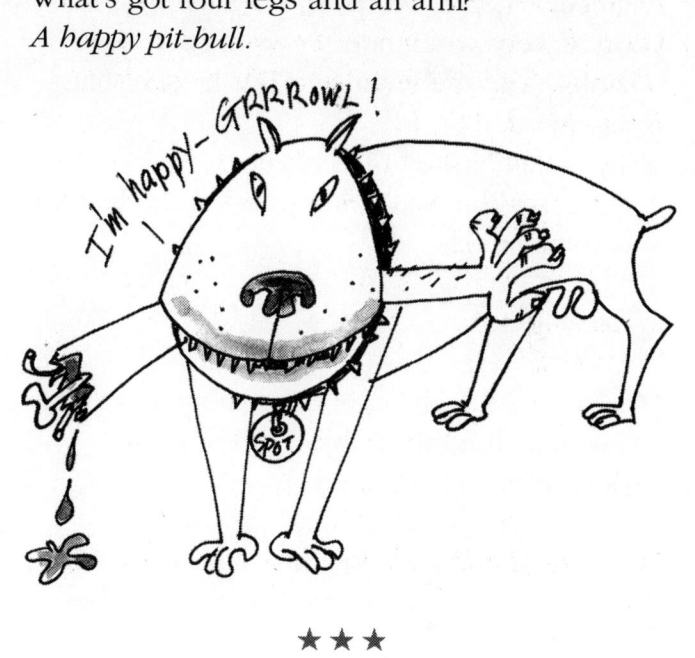

★ ★ ★

One night there was a terrible accident at a railway crossing. A train smashed into a car and pushed it half a mile down the track. Though no one was killed, the driver sued the train company. At the trial, the engineer insisted he had given the car driver ample warning by waving his lantern back and forth for at least thirty seconds. He even stood up and demonstrated how he'd done it. The jury believed his story and the lawsuit was dismissed.

'Congratulations,' said the lawyer to the

engineer when it was over. 'You handled yourself very well under cross-examination.'
'Thanks,' said the engineer. 'But he sure had me worried.'
'Why is that?' asked the lawyer.
'I was afraid he was going to ask if the lantern was blimmin' lit!'

★ ★ ★

Having lunch with one of her snottier authors, the editor raised the subject of the book review in the local paper.
'So,' she said to the author, 'do you know what the critic had to say about your book?'
'I have no idea, whatsoever,' said the author.
The editor replied, 'Well, more or less.'

★ ★ ★

The drunk said to his friend on a street corner one night, 'You know, I'll never forget the first time I turned to the bottle as a substitute for women.'
'Why?' asked his friend. 'What happened?'
The drunk replied, 'I got my penis stuck and needed a cork remover.'

★ ★ ★

Oddities

Sick and tired of his name-dropping friend Louis, who was always boasting about how well-connected he was, Eric said, 'Hey, buddy, if you're such a big shot, go over to the phone and call Nicole Kidman.'

Shrugging, Louis walked over to the phone, dialled a number and handed the phone to Eric.

'Hello,' came a voice that could be no one but the lovely Nicole, 'this is Nic speaking.'

Eric said, 'Okay, that was impressive, but if you're really such a hotshot, why don't you call Buckingham Palace and get the Queen to speak to me.'

With a bored sigh Louis dialled a number and gave the phone to Eric.

'Hello,' came a voice that could be no one but Her Majesty, 'This is the Queen of England speaking.'

Even though he was now very impressed, Eric was still a bit suspicious.

'All right, buddy, so you know Nicole Kidman and the Queen. But if you're really a big shot, you'll get the Pope on the phone.'

Promising to do even better than that, Louis drove Eric to the airport, and bought them tickets to the Vatican. There, Louis disappeared and Eric stood about, mingling with the crowd in St Peter's Square. Suddenly, the crowd fell into a reverent silence as they

all looked at the balcony, where Louis and the Pope stood side by side.
Before Eric could recover from the shock of seeing his mate up there, a man standing beside him poked him in the ribs. 'Hey, bud,' he said. 'Who's that guy up there with Louis?'

★ ★ ★

While eating at a restaurant, Mr and Mrs Jamison looked at each other in disgust as the trucker sitting next to them let out an enormous belch. Tapping his shoulder indignantly, Mr Jamison said, 'How dare you belch like that before my wife!' Looking up from his chilli, the trucker says, 'Sorry, mate, I didn't know it was her turn.'

★ ★ ★

How many evolutionists does it take to screw in a light bulb?
Just one, but it takes him 600,000 years.

★ ★ ★

John had committed a terrible crime and had been sentenced to death by electrocution. Just before he was led to the chair John was visited by the chaplain. 'They are going to

Oddities

allow you ten minutes of grace,' he said.
John shrugged. 'That ain't very long, but what the Hell. Send her in.'

★ ★ ★

How does a leper get out of a poker game?
He throws in his hand.

★ ★ ★

To succeed in medicine nowadays, every doctor needs two things,' said the professor to his medical students. 'The first is grey hair. That will make you look wise and responsible.'
'And the second thing?' asked a student.
'Haemorrhoids,' the instructor said, 'to give you a look of concern.'

★ ★ ★

Mr Webb, head of a local charity, was irritated because Mr Somers, one of the wealthiest men in town, still had not given his charity a donation. Mr Webb rang Mr Somers in order to give it his last shot. 'Sir, it is well known throughout this town that you're exceedingly wealthy. Would you be so kind as to share your good fortune with our organisation so

that we can continue helping those in need?'
Mr Somers replied, 'Listen. Is it also known throughout this town that I have a widowed, dying mother who has no source of income? Or a sister whose husband was killed and she now has five children to support? Or a brother who lost both arms and legs in a bad car accident?' He paused. 'And, if I don't give my money to them, why should I give it to you?'

★ ★ ★

Jay had been looking forward to his first skydiving class for ages.
'Now, class,' said the instructor, 'you've got to jump, count to ten, then pull the ripcord.'
Jay was so excited that he wasn't really paying close attention. He said, 'P-p-p-p-pardon m-m-me, wh-wh-wh-what w-w-was th-th-that n-n-n-number ag-ag-again?'
'Two,' the instructor replied.

★ ★ ★

The teacher was teaching her class about adjectives. 'Pick an adjective, and use it in a sentence,' she instructed.
Brittany calls out, 'Red. The rose is red.'
'Well done,' the teacher said. 'Marty, what about you?'

Oddities

'Broken,' said Marty. 'The window is broken.'
'Well done, Marty. Now Cody, your turn. Can you give me an adjective?'
'Urinate,' said the Cody.
'Cody!' she yelled. 'How could you?'
'What's the problem?' he replied. 'Urinate, but if you had your boobs done, you'd be a ten.'

★ ★ ★

'Waiter,' the customer said. 'How do you serve shrimps?'
The waiter replied, 'We bend down, sir.'

★ ★ ★

'Waiter,' said the customer. 'Why isn't there any soup on the menu?'
The waiter explained, 'I wiped it off.'

★ ★ ★

A kid came home from his first day at school. His mother asked, 'What did you learn today, sweetheart?'
'Obviously not enough,' snapped the boy, 'because they want me to go back tomorrow!'

★ ★ ★

Paddy was telling Seamus about his big brush with the law.
'You see, I got pulled over by a copper and he said, "Can you identify yourself?".'
'Strike me down! So what did you do?' gasped Seamus.
'Well,' smiled Paddy, 'I looked in the rear-vision mirror and said, "Yeah. That's me!".'

★ ★ ★

At the supermarket, a young boy and his mother were waiting in the check-out line behind an extremely obese fellow. Suddenly, the man's pager went off.
'Shit!' the kid screeched, 'Look out, Mum! The fat bastard's backing up!'

★ ★ ★

What's the one thing you shouldn't mumble after sex with your wife?
Do you take MasterCard?

★ ★ ★

How does a spoiled rich blonde change a light bulb?
She says, 'Daddy! I want a new apartment!'

★ ★ ★

Oddities

Rangi's wife Marama was so ugly that she spent eight hours in the beauty salon - and that was just for the quote.

★ ★ ★

How did Pinocchio find out that he was made of wood?
The first time he jerked off his hand caught fire.

★ ★ ★

Trying to make friends with his new cellmate, one criminal said to the other, 'I suppose you're going to have a hot time when you're through with this place!'
'I reckon you'd be right there,' replied the other criminal. 'I'm in for life.'

★ ★ ★

Feeling a little bit toey, a drunk decided to visit a prostitute. Unfortunately he was so inebriated that he mistakenly walked into a podiatrist's office. Winking lewdly at the receptionist, he said, 'Hey love, ya know what I'm here for!' She said she did, and told him to go into the doctor's office, sit on the examining table, and place his extremity on

the extension.
The drunk did as he was told, unzipping his fly and putting his privates on the cushion. When the nurse came back in, she yelled, 'Hey, that's not a foot!' Looking perplexed, the drunk said, 'Since when is there a minimum?'

★ ★ ★

When do masochists laugh?
Whenever anything strikes them funny.

★ ★ ★

Why were the lepers kicked off the rugby team?
Because they were defeated.

★ ★ ★

Memo to Employees
Lonesome?
Like to meet new people?
Like a change, a challenge?
Enjoy excitement, a change of scenery?
Like a new job?
Then just screw up one more time!

★ ★ ★

Oddities

Once upon a time, there was a little bird who decided not to fly to warmer areas for the winter as his little birdie friends did. He waved goodbye to his mates as they headed for the North Island and flew around by himself. However, the weather started to get colder and colder and grew so cold that the bird decided that he would have to head to the North Island after all, because it was too damn cold.

He had been flying for just a short while, however, when it began to snow. He collected so much snow on his wings that he began to freeze, and soon his wings grew too heavy to flap them. He fell to Earth in a farmyard, very close to death. A few seconds after he landed, a cow passed by and pooped all over the bird. The bird thought that this was surely the end, but the dung was warm and gently defrosted his wings. Warm and happy, the bird started to sing. Just then a big black cat came by and, hearing the bird chirping merrily away, it came closer to investigate, it meowed, 'Little bird, don't cry! I'm here for you!' However, very soon after that, the cat had a full belly, and the little birdie had gone to the Great Bird Aviary in the sky.

The moral of this story?

1. Everyone who shits on you is not your enemy.

2. Everyone who gets you out of the shit is not your friend.
3. If you're warm and happy in a pile of shit, keep your stupid mouth shut!

★ ★ ★

A Few Definitions...
A woman in love: A woman who divorces her husband.
A cynic: A person who tries to make everyone else's life as awful as his own.
Childhood: The brief (and rapidly shrinking) interval between the 'oh-what-a-cute-baby' comments and the first arrest on a drug charge.
Psychiatrist: A guy who goes to a nudie club and watches the customers.
Consciousness: Those annoying times between naps.

★ ★ ★

Dennis is an experienced sky-diver and is getting ready for his next jump. He spots a blind guy holding his guide dog who also appears ready to jump. Den is very impressed, but also quite concerned.
'I'm sorry to ask you this, and I must say from the outset that I consider you very brave – but

Oddities

how do you know when the ground is getting closer?' asks Dennis.
'Oh, that's easy!' exclaims the blind man, 'Gypsy's leash goes slack.'

★ ★ ★

Pinky is at work when one of his co-workers, Tommy, notices that Pinky is wearing an earring. Tommy knows that Pinky is a pretty conservative kind of bloke, so he is curious about the change.
'I didn't know you were into earrings,' he yells across the warehouse.
'Don't make such a big deal out of it,' hisses Pinky, embarrassed.
'No, really, mate. How long have you been into jewellery?' says Tommy.
'Ever since my wife found this earring in our bed.'

★ ★ ★

How do you get two little old ladies to yell out, 'Aw, @#$%!'
Have another little old lady yell out, 'House!'

★ ★ ★

225

More Great Kiwi Jokes

What did the elephant say to the naked man?
That's cute, but can it pick up peanuts?

★ ★ ★

Miss Underwood was organising an end-of-year pageant for her seven-year-old pupils. Some of the kids were to sing songs, and others were to tap dance, play musical instruments or recite poetry that they had written. However, little Jordan was a shy boy with no apparent talents. So, the teacher took him aside and said, 'Jordan, what do you like to do when you go home, after school'.
'Well, miss, I like to play with me Playstation. But I sometimes help me folks out on the farm,' he replied.
'Well, Jordan,' Miss Underwood smiled, 'your task for our pageant is to make farmyard noises.' So it was settled.

Oddities

The pageant rolled around – little Susie had done her tap dance, and little Bobby had played his clarinet. Then it was Jordan's turn. 'Farmyard noises,' he timidly announced to the audience of kids, parents and teachers. Cupping his mouth, the little boy bellowed like a fishmonger: 'Oi! Will ya get off that f***ing tractor? Shut that f***ing gate! Get that f***ing sheep out of the yard...'

★ ★ ★

More Great Kiwi Jokes

Ever Wondered...?

- If homeless people get knock knock jokes?
- Why we say something 'is out of whack', what's a whack?
- Why the man who invests all your money is called a broker?
- Why croutons come in airtight packages? They're just stale bread to begin with.
- What cheese says when it gets its picture taken?
- Why if someone tells you there are one billion stars in the universe you will believe them. But if they tell you a wall has wet paint, you have to touch it to be sure?
- Why when you know something is going to smell really bad, you can't resist taking a whiff?
- What the speed of lightning would be if it didn't zigzag?
- If milk comes out of a cow's nose when she laughs?

★ ★ ★

An attractive young woman went to the gynaecologist for an examination. While examining her, the doctor asks, 'So, have you had a check-up here before?'
Looking a little puzzled, she tentatively replies,

Oddities

'Noooo. But I have had a German or two, a Russian and some Polish bloke.'

★ ★ ★

James the little farm boy from Timaru comes down to breakfast when his mother asks him if he's done his chores. 'Not yet, Mum,' says James, to which his mother replies, 'No chores, no breakfast.'
Off he goes in a pissed-off mood. He kicks a chicken while feeding the chooks, and kicks a cow during his milking duties. As he is feeding the pigs, he decides to kick one of the piglets.
On James' return, his mother serves him a bowl of dry cereal.
'Where's the milk?' he squawks, 'And what about my bacon and eggs?'
'Listen, James,' says his mother, 'I saw you kick the chicken, so no eggs for you. And you also booted the poor little piglet, so no bacon. Likewise, you get no milk because of kicking the helpless cow.'
Just then, his father comes down for breakfast and kicks the cat off his chair.
Little Jimmy looks up at his mum and says, 'Are you going to tell him or should I?'

★ ★ ★

After weeks of abdominal pain and a multitude of tests, the ailing patient returns to his doctor for the results.

'Hmmnnn,' mutters the doctor looking up from his paperwork. 'I have good news and I have bad news.'

The patient, obviously concerned, sighs, 'I suppose I'd better have the good news first,'

'Well,' beams the doc, 'We're going to name a disease after you.'

★ ★ ★

One night as a couple lay in bed, the husband gently taps his wife on the shoulder and becomes a little amorous.

'Not tonight, dear,' sighs the woman sleepily, 'I've got a gynaecologist's appointment tomorrow and I need to stay fresh.'

Rejected, he turns over and tries to sleep.

A few minutes later, he taps his wife on the shoulder again. This time he whispers, 'You aren't going to the dentist tomorrow, are you?'

★ ★ ★

A renowned heart surgeon dies and at his funeral his coffin rests in front of a huge heart on the crematorium wall. After the minister finishes his sermon, and after everybody has

Oddities

said their goodbyes to the deceased, the heart is opened and the coffin rolled inside. The heart then closes, and the coffin is whisked off.

Just at that moment, one of the mourners starts laughing hysterically. The guy beside him exclaims, 'Why on Earth would you be laughing in a moment like this?'

'I was thinking about my own funeral,' the man chortles.

'And what's so funny about that?' puzzles the bloke beside him.

'I'm a gynaecologist!'

★ ★ ★

Two Aussie Siamese twins go to the same resort in southern France every year and have been doing so for fifteen years. Not surprisingly, the head waiter at a popular restaurant in the resort town recognizes them.

'Is it the weather that keeps bringing you back?' he asks.

'Oh, no!' replies one of the twins, 'We burn very easily.'

'Perhaps you are wine connoisseurs, then?' wonders the waiter.

'No, no,' says the other twin, 'we are strictly beer drinkers.'

'I know,' says the waiter, 'it must be our

wonderful French cuisine.'
'Actually,' the twins say, shaking their heads in unison, 'we're fish and chips boys any day!'
'So what could possibly make you come back here year after year?' asks the puzzled waiter.
'Well,' says one twin, 'It's the only chance my brother gets to drive!'

★ ★ ★

A stockbroker parks his new Porsche in front of the office to show it off to his colleagues. Just as he is getting out of the car, an out-of-control semi-trailer comes flying along and takes off the door before speeding off. The stockbroker phones the police on his mobile. When the officer arrives five minutes later, the stockbroker is distraught. 'My Porsche! My beautiful silver Porsche is ruined! No matter how long it's at the panel-beaters, it will never be the same again!'
After he finally stops ranting, the policeman shakes his head in disgust. 'You rich pricks really piss me off!' he exclaims. 'You are so materialistic and focused on your possessions that you don't notice anything else, do you?'
'How can you say such a thing at a time like this,' snaps the broker.
'Mate, you didn't even notice that your right arm was torn off by the truck, too!' blurts the

Oddities

copper in disbelief.
The stockbroker looks down in absolute horror, 'Oh, f***!' he screams, 'Where's my bloody Rolex!'

★ ★ ★

For a class project, the kindergarten teacher asks her pupils what, out of any material in the world, they would like to be made of.
Quickly, Trent shoots his arm up. 'I would like to be made of gold, miss!' he squeaks. 'Then I could scratch my arm and use a few flakes of gold to buy a new Skyline GTR.'
Then little Courtenay pipes up, too, 'Nah, miss,' he cries, 'I'd like to be made of platinum, cos it's worth more than gold and I could use a few flakes of it to buy two new cars!'
'And what about you, Tyco?' asks the teacher.
'Simple, miss. Pubic hair is the answer,' says little Tyco.
'Why on Earth would you want to be made of that?!' shrieks the teacher, aghast.
'Well, my sister's only got a little bit left,' Tyco replies, 'but you should see how many cars we've got outside our house.'

★ ★ ★

More Great Kiwi Jokes

A young man in his brand new HSV Commodore stops at a red light. An old man on a Vespa pulls up beside him.
'That's a beaut car, sonny! Mind if I have a look inside?' and with that the old codger pokes his head through the window and takes a look around. 'Nice car, alright. But I'll stick to my scooter!'
The young man, brazen as a bull, decides to show the old bloke just what his car is capable of doing. Within seconds, the speedo reads 160km/h.
Suddenly, the kid notices a dot in his rear-view mirror, then something roars past him. Not to be outdone, he buries his boot and gazes toward the horizon. He's astonished to see that it's the old bloke on the Vespa who is ahead of him! Amazed, he speeds up to 200km/h and passes the Vespa. But when he checks his rear-view mirror again, he sees that the old man is gaining on him. He floors it again and gets up to 260km/h, but the Vespa is still coming!
Suddenly, the scooter ploughs right into the back of the brand new Holden. The young bloke jumps out quickly to see if the old fella is still alive.
He runs up to him sprawled on the ground and stammers in horror, 'Oh-h G-god! Is there anything I can do?'

Oddities

The old guy shrieks, 'Yes, you little f***wit! You can unhook my braces from your wing mirror!'

★ ★ ★

For Any Occasion

A woman takes a lover while her husband is at work. Her nine-year-old son comes home from school unexpectedly, so she puts him in the wardrobe and shuts the door. Her husband also comes home unexpectedly, so she shoves her lover in the wardrobe with the little boy.
The little boy says, 'Gee, it's dark in here.'
The man replies, 'Sure is.'
The little boy says, 'I have a cricket bat.'
The man replies, 'Good for you.'
The little boy says, 'Want to buy it?'
The man replies, 'No, thanks.'
The little boy says, 'My dad's outside.'
Catching his drift, the man replies, 'Okay, how much?'
The little boy says, '$250.'
The next week, it happens that the boy and his mum's lover are in the wardrobe together again.

For Any Occasion

The little boy says, 'Gee, it's dark in here.'
The man replies, 'Yep.'
The little boy says, 'I have some wickets.'
The man, remembering the last time, sniffs, 'Right. How much?'
The little boy says, '$750.'
The man grimaces, 'Fine.'
On the weekend, the boy is up in his room playing with his brand new Playstation when his dad bursts in and says, 'Okay, kiddo. Grab your cricket gear. Let's go outside for a bit of hit-to-hit.'
The little boy says, 'Sorry, I can't, Dad. I sold my gear.'
His father replies, 'What? How much did you sell it for?'
'$1000.'
The father says, 'What?! Not only was your cricket gear a Christmas present, but it's terrible to overcharge your friends like that. You, my boy, are going to church to confess.'
So, they go to church and the father shoves his son into the confession booth.
After a few moments, the little boy says, 'Gee, it's dark in here.'
The priest says, 'Don't you bloody start that again!'

★★★

A man and his wife are wakened at three o'clock in the morning by a loud pounding on the door. The man gets up and goes to the door. A drunken stranger is standing in the pouring rain, and asks him for a push.
'Not a chance, pal,' says the husband. 'It's bloody three o'clock in the morning!' And he slams the door and returns to bed.
'Who was it, sweetheart?' asks his wife.
'Just a drunken stranger asking for a push,' he answers.
'And did you help him?' she asks.
'I certainly did not. It's three o'clock in the morning and pouring with rain.'
'Well, you've got a short memory,' snorts his wife. 'Can't you remember about three months ago when we broke down on holiday and those two guys helped us out? I think you should get back out there and help him.'
The man does as he is told. He gets dressed and goes out in the pouring rain and calls out into the dark, 'Hello, are you still there?'
'Yes,' comes the answer.
'Do you still want a push?' calls out the husband.
'Yes, please!' comes the reply from the dark.
'Fine. But where are you?' asks the husband.
'Over here, on the swing,' the drunk replies.

★ ★ ★

For Any Occasion

There were two brothers who were utter ratbags. Whenever something went wrong in their neighbourhood, it turned out that they had a hand in it. Their parents were at their wits' end trying to control them. Hearing about a minister nearby who worked with delinquent boys, the mother suggested that they ask the minister to talk with the boys. The father agreed.

The mother went to the minister and made her request. He agreed, but said he wanted to see the younger boy first. So the mother sent him to the minister. The minister sat the boy down on the other side of his huge, impressive desk. For about five minutes they just sat and stared at each other. Finally, the minister pointed his forefinger at the boy and asked, 'Where is God?'

The boy looked under the desk, in the corners of the room, all around, but said nothing.

Again, louder, the minister pointed at the boy and asked, 'Where is God?' Again the boy looked all around, but said nothing. A third time, in a louder, firmer voice, the minister leaned far across the desk and put his forefinger almost to the boy's nose, and boomed, 'WHERE IS GOD?'

The boy panicked and ran all the way home. Finding his older brother, he dragged him

upstairs to their room and into the wardrobe, where they usually plotted their mischief. He finally simpered, 'Bro, we are in BIG trouble now!'
The older boy scoffed, 'What do you mean, BIG trouble?'
His brother replied, 'God's gone missing and they think it's our fault.'

★ ★ ★

Two little boys were overheard chatting at kindergarten one day.
'Hello, I'm Corey. What's your name?' asked the first boy.
'Jeremy,' replied the second.
'My daddy's a mechanic. What does your daddy do for a living?' asked Corey.
Jeremy replied, 'Dad's a lawyer.'
'Honest?' asked Corey.
'Nah, just the regular kind.'

★ ★ ★

A priest, a doctor, and a lawyer were waiting one morning on a particularly slow group of golfers on the green.
'What's bloody wrong with these guys?' fumed the lawyer. 'We must have been waiting for 15 minutes!'

For Any Occasion

'I don't know,' said the doctor, 'but I've never seen such ineptitude!'
'Fellas, here comes the groundsman,' said the priest. 'Say, groundsman, what's the problem with that group ahead of us? They're rather slow, aren't they?'
'Oh, yes,' said groundsman, 'that's the group of blind firefighters. They lost their sight while saving our clubhouse last year. We let them play here any time, free of charge!'
Everyone was silent for a moment.
Then the priest said, 'That's so sad, I think I'll say a prayer for them tonight.'
'And I'm going to contact my ophthalmologist buddy and see if there is anything he can do for them,' the doctor added.
'Yeah, yeah. But why can't these guys play at night?' asked the lawyer.

★ ★ ★

A man in Nelson calls his adult son in Auckland and says, 'Steve, I hate to ruin your day, but I have to tell you that your mother and I are divorcing; thirty-two years of misery is quite enough.'
Steve is hysterical. 'Dad, what are you talking about?' he screams.
'Your mum and I, we can't stand the sight of each other any longer,' his old man says.

'We're sick of each other, and I'm sick of talking about this, so you call your sister in Wellington and tell her,' and with that he hangs up.

Frantic, Steve calls his sister, who explodes on the phone.

'Like heck they're getting divorced,' she shouts, 'I'll take care of this.'

She calls her dad immediately and shrieks, 'Dad! You are NOT getting divorced! Don't do a single thing until I get there. I'm calling Steve back, and we'll both be there tomorrow. Until then, don't do a thing, DO YOU HEAR ME?' She then slams down the phone.

The man turns to his wife.

'Darling,' he chuckles, 'the kids are coming home for Christmas *and* paying their own airfares.'

★ ★ ★

The priest was preparing a man for his long day's journey into night. Whispering firmly, the priest said, 'Denounce the devil! Let him know how little you think of him!'

The dying man said nothing.

The priest repeated his order.

Still, the man said nothing.

The priest pleaded, 'My friend, why do you refuse to denounce the devil and his evil?'

For Any Occasion

The dying man rasped, 'Mate, until I know for sure where I'm heading, I don't think I ought to aggravate anybody.'

★ ★ ★

A lady was walking down the street to work, and she saw a parrot on a perch in front of a pet shop. The parrot squawked to her, 'Hey lady, you are really ugly.'
Well, the lady is furious, and stormed past the shop.
On the way home, she saw the same parrot and it squawked to her again, 'Hey lady, you are really ugly.' She was incredibly ticked off now, and walked away in a huff.
The next day as she passed the pet shop, the same parrot said to her, 'Hey lady, you are really ugly.'
The lady was so incensed that she whorled into the pet shop in a cyclone of fury. Virtually foaming at the mouth, she threatened that she would sue the store and kill the bird if it humiliated her like that ever again. The store manager apologised profusely, and promised to ensure that the parrot would cease being so offensive.
When the lady walked past the pet shop that day after work, the parrot called to her, 'Hey lady.'

She paused and grimaced, 'Yes?'
The bird said, 'Awww, shucks, you know what I'm gonna say...'

★ ★ ★

Early one evening, a middle-aged bloke scuttled outside and pulled the garden furniture out onto the driveway. Shortly after followed the lawnmower, a few tools and a bicycle, all strewn across the driveway. A curious neighbour wandered over and asked if he was going to have a garage sale.
'Nah,' replied the bloke, 'my son just bought his first car and he's inside getting ready for a big date.'
'Right. So what's with all the stuff?' asked the puzzled neighbour.
'Well, after years of moving tricycles, toys and sports equipment out of the way every time I came home from work, I wanted to make sure that the driveway was ready for him.'

★ ★ ★

Different Engineering Perspectives
Four men rode in a car: a mechanical engineer, an electrical engineer, a chemical engineer, and a computer engineer.
The car stalled.

For Any Occasion

The mechanical engineer said, 'It must be the pistons; let's repair them and be on our way.'
The electrical engineer said, 'Nah, it has to be the spark plugs; we'll replace them and be ready to roll in no time at all.'
The chemical engineer said, 'Sorry fellas, but it has got to be a problem with the fuel; we'll flush the system and then get going.'
Considering everyone in the car had an opinion, they turned to the computer engineer, thinking that he was probably the smartest of the lot.
'So, what do you think we should do?' they asked.
The computer engineer shrugged and replied, 'I reckon, let's get out of the car, close the doors, then get back in and try restarting it.'

★ ★ ★

The flight from Auckland to Los Angeles is out on the runway, and all the passengers are seated expectantly in their seats. The cabin crew have demonstrated the air-safety instructions, and everyone is just waiting, twiddling their thumbs, really.
With their birds-eye view of the plane, the passengers in business class can see that the pilots' cabin is empty. Neither the pilot nor co-pilot have shown up.

More Great Kiwi Jokes

Moments before the scheduled take-off, two blind jokers in pilot costumes turn up. As they bumble their way down the aisle, knocking into things, the passengers all laugh, thinking that the airline has decided to provide some light relief before the long haul over to the States.

However, the men eventually make it to the cabin and shut the door behind them. The seatbelt signal is on, and the engines begin to roar. Next thing, the plane is off, tearing up the tarmac. The problem is that it is going the wrong way; the plane is heading back towards the terminal at frightening speeds. Looking at their loved ones who had waved them off through the plated glass, the passengers begin to scream. They are about to crash into the airport!

In a blink of an eye, the plane smoothly lifts up out and into the ether, bound for LA.

'Jesus!' comes a surly voice crackling over the pilots' intercom to the mortified passengers. 'One of these days you guys are going to scream too late, and we'll all be rooted!'

★ ★ ★

For Any Occasion

Looking for something a little different to do on Saturday morning, Bob headed into a magic shop, looking for some tricks to impress his grandkids with. After he picked up a few gismos and gadgets for the youngsters, he noticed some x-ray vision glasses that could possibly be entertaining for himself. Sure enough, after he put the glasses on, all of the sales staff appeared starkers. Thinking that he could certainly have some fun with these glasses, Bob hastily purchased them, and decided to rush around to his best mate's place to show off.

After an entertaining drive through the suburbs wearing x-ray vision glasses, Bob burst through the front door of his best mate's place, screaming 'taa-daa!'.

There, lying naked on the sofa, was Bob's wife with his very own best mate.

Taking his glasses off to explain to them that he had purchased some excellent new x-ray vision glasses, Bob noticed that his missus and his best mate were still naked, not to mention looking rather shocked.

'Oh, bloody hell! I can't believe it either! After just half an hour, these x-ray vision glasses have permanently skewed my vision!'

★ ★ ★

Two blokes were standing at the urinal together. Rob peered over to Greg and was astounded to see his endowment.
'Christ! That thing is monstrous, you lucky bastard!' he gushed jealously.
'Yeah,' smirked Greg, 'But I've got to admit that I wasn't always so impressive to the ladies. I had a penile transplant performed a few years back. It cost two thousand bucks, but I say it's worth every dollar.'
Thinking that he wouldn't mind a bit more action, Rob asked the name of the cosmetic surgeon who had performed Greg's procedure.
A few months later, the blokes bumped into each other, once again at the urinal.
Rob smiled, 'I see that your penis is still serving you well. You might have noticed that I too got a transplant.'
'Hmmmnnnn, not bad,' replied Greg, having a bit of a gander. 'So how much did he charge you for that one?'
'Well, it was half price – I only paid $1000 for my whopper,' skited Rob.
'Yeah, I can see why,' came the reply 'you've wound up with my old one.'

★ ★ ★

For Any Occasion

It was early in the morning at the casino, and a gorgeous woman walked over to one of the craps tables where two dealers were standing bored and waiting for custom. She said that she had money to burn, and wanted to bet fifty thousand dollars on a single roll of the dice.

'Sure thing, lady' replied one of the dealers, smirking at the other.

'Great,' she cooed, 'however, I will do this on one condition. You must allow me to remove my skirt and underpants before I roll the dice.'

The dealers were both dumbfounded, and could barely nod their heads in the affirmative.

So, the woman whipped of her skirt and knickers and rolled the dice.

'Woohoo! I've won!' she squealed. Then she scooped up the chips, grabbed her clothing and streaked out the door.

The two dealers stood there in stunned silence. 'So what did she roll, anyway?' said one to the other.

'Crikey, I don't know! I thought you were watching the dice.'

★ ★ ★

Barry was overweight. He had tried every crash diet available, but just couldn't seem to move the kilos. One day, as he was tucking into a huge portion of fish n' chips, he noticed on the wrapper an advertisement for yet another diet clinic. 'Sex Diet. Lose Kilos the Fun Way!'

Without a moments hesitation, Barry shoved another potato cake in his mouth, and called the 'Sex Diet' hot line. The woman who answered advised that it cost $20 for each ten kilograms of weight he lost. Barry had about 30 kilograms to lose, and decided to go for it, relaying his credit card details over the line. 'Right, tonight just after dinner, one of our gorgeous women will knock on your door.'

Sure enough, as soon as he'd tucked away his last piece of fried chicken for the evening, there came a knock at the door. On his doorstep was a stunning redhead in a PVC tracksuit.

'Okay, honey,' she snapped. 'You catch me, you screw me.' And with that, she bolted down the street. Barry huffed and puffed for a good hour or so, running around the suburb, and he didn't catch her. However, by the time he got home, his extreme energy expended whilst chasing this bodacious babe had depleted an amazing ten kilograms from his frame.

For Any Occasion

The next week, Barry made another phone call to the 'Sex Diet' hotline. 'Right, I lost ten kilos, now I'd like to lose another ten!' he panted down the line.
'Sure. But the price has gone up. The second ten kilos costs $200,' came the reply.
'Aaah, why not,' smiled Barry, knowing that every dollar was worth it.
Sure enough, once he'd finished off his second pizza that night, there came a knock at the door. On his doorstep was a ravishing brunette in a PVC tracksuit.
'Here goes, sweetheart,' she smirked. 'You catch me, you screw me.' And with that, she bolted down the street. Barry huffed and puffed for a good hour or so, running around the suburb, and he didn't catch her. However, by the time he got home, the extreme energy expended whilst chasing this foxy filly, had depleted an amazing ten kilograms from his frame.
The next week, Barry made another phone call to the 'Sex Diet' hotline. 'Right, I lost another ten kilos, now I'd like to lose yet another ten!' he panted down the line.
'Sure. But the third ten kilos is going to cost you $2000,' came the reply.
'That's cool,' chuckled Barry, knowing that this time he was fitter and faster than ever before. He'd definitely catch whichever vixen they

made him chase.

Sure enough, once he'd finished off his tray of nachos that night, there came a knock at the door. But this time on his doorstep was the fattest, ugliest, most repulsive woman he had ever seen.

'Okey-doke,' she leered, 'I paid good money to catch you. If I can, I can screw you... '

★ ★ ★

Three women turned up for a job interview. The human resources officer who was holding the interview had no ears, and was rather paranoid about the way it made him look. So, in a slight abuse of power, he would only hire people that he considered accepting of his condition.

He told the first candidate, 'Now, this job calls for a discerning and perceptive nature. What was the first thing you noticed about me?'

'Er... mister... you have no ears,' came the nervous reply.

'Get out of my office!' the human resources officer screamed, shoving the candidate's resume back in her hand.

Then, the next candidate came in to be interviewed.

'Okay, this job calls for a discerning and perceptive nature. Tell me, what was the first

For Any Occasion

thing that you noticed about me?'
'Simple. You are one earless mother,' came the rather brash reply.
'Get out of my office!' screamed the HR officer, taking a gush from his asthma pump in an attempt to calm down.
Finally, the third candidate came in to be interviewed.
'Tell me, ma'am. This job requires someone with a discerning and perceptive nature. What was the first thing you noticed about me?'
'You wear contact lenses,' came the reply.
This was music to the human resources officer's ears (or lack thereof). Finally, he had found a candidate who hadn't been biased toward his disability, and could just see him as he was.
'Hallelujah!' he gushed. 'I do wear contact lenses. How on Earth did you notice such a thing?'
'Well, you certainly couldn't wear glasses.'

★ ★ ★

A beautiful young woman was gazing wistfully through the window of a designer shoe store, when the smarmy sales fellow beckoned her inside. Hesitantly, she walked in. 'Sir, I'm only browsing,' she explained, 'to be honest, I couldn't afford a thing in this store.'

'Well, that may be the case,' he said, raising his eyebrow, 'but I'm willing to give you those shoes for just twenty dollars.'

'Twenty dollars!' she shrieked. 'But they are worth at least $800!'

'True,' nodded the salesman, 'the one condition of this sale is that you have sex with me. Do so, and those gorgeous specimens of style, glamour and chic are yours, babe.'

The girl couldn't help herself, 'Oh, okay,' she sighed, 'but I must warn you, I don't enjoy sex. It doesn't do a thing for me, so don't be offended if I seem disinterested.'

So he gave her the shoes, and they headed out into the back room. He busied himself away, while she just lay there passively, snapping gum. Suddenly, she ecstatically threw her legs up in the air, writhed and squealed, 'Wonderful! Magnificent! Divine! Oh dear God, this is just so fabulous!'

Perplexed, he gasped, 'But I thought you didn't enjoy having sex?'

'Oh, I don't,' giggled the woman, 'I'm just admiring these gorgeous new shoes!'

★ ★ ★

The lawyer's rottweiler escapes from its lead and runs amok through the suburban streets. Finally, it comes to rest at the local

For Any Occasion

meatologist, and swipes a huge leg of lamb from the dismayed butcher's clutches.

The lawyer came panting in and said, 'Sorry, pal, that's my dog.'

'You! You're a lawyer, right,' replied the butcher.

'Yes,' answered the lawyer.

'Well, if some bastard's dog comes running salivating into my hygienic shop and swipes a leg of lamb clean from my hand, I've got every right to charge him for that leg of lamb, don't I?'

'Yes,' seethed the lawyer, writing the butcher a cheque for twenty dollars.

As the lawyer left the shop, the butcher placed the cheque into the cash register. However, on the other side of the cheque he noticed the words, 'Consultation: $50'

★ ★ ★

A woman went to a psychiatrist to try and sort out her problematic sex life. She went on and on for over an hour about how frustrated she was becoming, and how sex with her husband was always such a let down. She just didn't know why she was bothering to make the effort.

'I see,' replied the psychiatrist. 'From what you have told me, I think that the problem here is

a lack of communication. Tell me, do you ever look at your husband right in the eye whilst you are making love?'
'Sure. But only once,' the woman shrugged.
'You see, ma'am, that's part of the problem. To only do that once in all your years of marriage, shows a distinct lack of tenderness. How did he look when you had this eye-to-eye contact?' he surmised.
'Ooooh, he was bloody furious!' remembered the woman.
'Furious? I see,' puzzled the psychiatrist. 'And what were the circumstances that would have made him furious? Fury is a curious emotion to have whilst lovemaking.'
'I agree,' responded the woman. 'But I should cut him some slack. After all, he was looking through the window at the time...'

★ ★ ★